Linda Collister

photography by Vanessa Davies

Cooking
with kids

RYLAND
PETERS
& SMALL

LONDON NEW YORK

Designer Catherine Griffin
Commissioning Editor Elsa Petersen-Schepelern
Production Deborah Werner
Art Director Gabriella Le Grazie
Publishing Director Alison Starling

Food Stylist Lucy McKelvie
Stylist Helen Trent
Indexer Hilary Bird

anks to my lovely, greedy kids

Originally published in hardback
in Great Britain in 2003

This paperback edition published in 2007
by Ryland Peters & Small
20–21 Jockey's Fields
London WC1R 4BW
www.rylandpeters.com

10 9 8 7 6 5 4 3 2 1

ISBN-13: 978 1 84597 488 6
ISBN-10: 184597 488 3

A CIP record for this book is available
from the British Library.

Author's acknowledgements
I would like to thank the following for their
help with this book:

Elsa Petersen-Schepelern, Catherine Griffin,
Vanessa Davies, Lucie McKelvie, Helen
Trent, Barbara Levy, Daniel, Stevie, Emily
and Alan Hertz, Emi Kazuko, Elaine
Hallgarten, Alyson Cook, Michelle Kershaw
and Lakeland Ltd, Simon Silverwood and
Alan Silverwood Ltd, the children and staff
of Darell School, Eve De Leon Allen, Emma
Greenwood, Scarlett Honey McKelvie,
Algernon and Stanley Mitchell,
Susannah and Olivia Nettleton and
Julia Niedertubbesing-Lopez.

Notes
All spoon measurements are level unless
otherwise specified.

All eggs are medium, unless otherwise
specified. Uncooked or partly cooked eggs
should not be served to the very young, the
very old, those with compromised immune
systems or to pregnant women.

Before baking, weigh or measure all
ingredients exactly and prepare baking tins
or sheets.

cooking with kids

contents

just for fun ...

I'm lucky – I have been surrounded by good food for as long as I can remember. My parents loved to travel and eat out, and saw no reason not to share that with us.

I didn't set out to teach my own children how to cook – they just joined in. Like my own parents, I could see no reason to stop them. I still can't.

Cooking as a family activity started when Emily was 18 months old. She sat in a corner of the kitchen, away from the business end, stirring a bowl of batter. Then from the majesty of her highchair she watched, agog, as pancakes sizzled on the griddle. Finally she got to eat the stack she had made, sticky with peanut butter and maple syrup! Now every Sunday begins with pancakes. All three children weigh, whisk, fold in egg whites, fry, flip and serve – they even set the table.

Planning meals and shopping for them are important, too. From watching and listening to my (admittedly fussy) mother-in-law at the butcher's, Daniel learned how to choose between different cuts of meat. When Stevie was going through her Think Pink stage at three, she would plan all pink meals. Her masterpiece was a warm salad of fresh borlotti beans, fresh cherries and grilled duck breasts with a raspberry vinaigrette. She got the idea when she was looking around our Italian greengrocer's shop.

So how do you get children involved? Start by picking a recipe or a menu together, then shopping together, paying careful attention to the ingredients. With very young children, try choosing fruit for a salad and asking which should be peeled, which have seeds, which don't need cutting up. Talk about where the fruits come from and why they are good for you.

In the kitchen, of course, you need some ground rules. These are just common sense, but they must be stated clearly and explained. Wash your hands, pull up long sleeves, tie back long hair, wear an apron. Make sure they understand that kitchen knives and other equipment are not toys, but can harm if not treated carefully, and that the stove can get very hot, so they should keep their distance.

Read the recipe through with the child before you start, so you both know what you are doing. Then get out all the equipment and ingredients. If possible, invest in a few pieces of child-friendly, good-quality equipment (not those kiddy-cooking packs from toy shops). Ideally, children should have their own vegetable peeler and vegetable knife with handles they can grip easily. A non-stick frying pan (not too heavy), non-stick baking and roasting trays, bowls with non-slip rubber bases, a rotary cheese-grater and rotary or electric whisk, plus a kitchen timer are all useful – and don't forget good oven gloves.

Decide which parts of the recipe your children can safely manage – you know their abilities best – then work together. Older children with cooking experience can usually get a cake in and out of the oven (remind them to use oven gloves), but straining a pan full of boiling pasta or vegetables is best done by an adult. Obviously, never leave a child alone in the kitchen while you are both cooking, and warn them not to make secret meals and snacks (though I'm sure I'm not the only mum who's been served an interesting breakfast in bed on Mother's Day).

I'm hoping that when my children finish primary school they can make, and enjoy, a good healthy meal for themselves. It would also be nice if they could use the washing machine, the vacuum cleaner, the garden rake and the duster – not just the computer.

little snacks

Children always arrive home from school starving, and need something to keep them going until supper appears – so these are ideas for them to make when they have to eat straight away! Sliced bread can quickly be turned into cinnamon toast (just buttered toast plus sugar and spice) or a filling toastie (really a fried cheese sandwich). Some snacks will keep, happily waiting for them – hoummus (a creamy, soft vegetarian pâté made with chickpeas) can be stored in the refrigerator overnight, and homemade ice lollies can stay in the freezer for a few weeks. No time at all? Then make a fruit smoothie in the blender.

The quickest treat yet invented – hot buttered toast sprinkled with cinnamon-flavoured sugar, then grilled until crunchy. Thick slices of bread, challah or brioche (two kinds of soft bread) work best, but you can also choose crumpets or English muffins split in half.

cinnamon toast

1 ASK AN ADULT to preheat the grill.

2 Toast the 2 slices of bread in a toaster. Carefully remove the hot toast from the toaster, then spread it with butter, using as much or as little as you like.

3 Mix the sugar with the cinnamon, then sprinkle it over the buttered toast to cover in an even layer. You could also put the mixture in an old sugar shaker, carefully screw on the top, then shake it over the toast.

4 ASK AN ADULT TO HELP YOU put the toast under the grill for 30 seconds to 1 minute until the sugar has melted and looks all bubbly, then carefully remove it.

5 Let cool for a minute (the sugar is very hot and will burn your lips) before eating.

2 thick slices of bread

unsalted butter

1½ tablespoons caster sugar

½ teaspoon ground cinnamon

SERVES 1 TO 2

This is the traditional way to make toasties – using a non-stick frying pan or electric frying pan. It makes the best, crunchiest, runniest sandwiches. You can use whatever filling you like.

grilled cheese sandwich

softened butter, for spreading

2 thick slices of bread

a slice of Cheddar or Swiss cheese (about 40 g)

SERVES 1

1 Butter one side of each piece of bread. Put the cheese on the unbuttered side of 1 piece of the bread, then cover with the second piece so the buttered side faces up (the reverse of a normal cheese sandwich).

2 ASK AN ADULT TO HELP YOU heat the frying pan to medium heat for a couple of minutes, then carefully put the sandwich in the pan. The butter will start sizzling straight away. Cook for 2 to 3 minutes until the underside is golden brown, then carefully turn the sandwich over with a spatula or fish slice. Cook the second side in the same way for 2 to 3 minutes.

3 Carefully lift the sandwich out of the pan and onto a plate. Cut in half, then eat.

Other ideas
• Add a slice of ham to the cheese filling – in France, this is called a *Croque Monsieur.*
• Add 2 or 3 slices of tomato or large mushroom.

Use your favourite hard cheese, such as Cheddar or Gruyère, then add extra ingredients as you fancy.

cheese melts

60 g cheese

½ teaspoon Dijon or mild mustard

a big pinch of freshly ground black pepper

1 teaspoon softened butter

MAKES 2 THICK SLICES

1 ASK AN ADULT TO HELP YOU heat the grill to its highest setting.

2 Toast the bread on both sides under the grill or in a toaster.

3 While the bread is toasting, grate the cheese with a rotary grater (or ordinary kitchen grater) into a small bowl.

4 Put the mustard, pepper and butter in the bowl and mix well with a small palette knife or a table knife.

5 Divide the cheese mixture in half, then spread one half on each slice of toast (if you want to make only one piece of cheese melt, cover the rest of the cheese mixture and keep in the refrigerator for up to 4 days).

6 Carefully put the cheese-covered toast under the hot grill and leave for 1 to 2 minutes until golden brown and bubbly. When cheese melts, its fats become very hot and can easily burn, so take great care as you lift it out of the grill, and ASK AN ADULT TO HELP. Let cool for a minute before eating.

Other ideas

• Put a slice of ham on top of the toast, spread with the cheese mixture, then grill.
• Spread about 1 tablespoon canned tuna (well-drained) over the toast, cover with the cheese mix, then grill (don't worry if it gets a bit mixed up).
• Put about 3 slices of tomato on top of the cheese mix on the toast before grilling.

This fruity salsa is delicious with Cheese Melts and also with Tortilla Chips (page 19).

fresh peach salsa

1 large ripe peach

3 cherry tomatoes

1 small lime

a few fresh coriander leaves or chives

a big pinch of crushed dried chillies

salt and freshly ground black pepper

SERVES 1 OR 2

1 Using a small sharp knife, carefully slice the peach in half from top to bottom. Twist the halves in opposite directions, then pull apart. Ease out the stone. Turn the peach halves flat side down on a chopping board and cut into small cubes. Put the pieces in a small bowl.

2 Cut each tomato in 4 and add to the bowl.

3 Cut the lime in half and squeeze out the juice with a lemon squeezer. Pour the lime juice over the peach and tomato pieces. Using kitchen scissors, snip the coriander leaves or chives into the bowl. Add the crushed chillies, salt and pepper and mix well with a small spoon. Taste, and add more chilli, salt or pepper as needed.

4 Eat immediately or cover and keep in the refrigerator for up to 4 hours.

hoummus

400 g canned chickpeas

2 tablespoons tahini paste

2 tablespoons olive oil

1 lemon

1 garlic clove

a small handful of parsley leaves

a big pinch of salt

a big pinch of ground black pepper

a big pinch of ground cumin

sweet paprika, for sprinkling

SERVES 4 TO 6

Hoummus is good for spreading on toast or warm pita breads, and also as a dip for carrot, cucumber and celery sticks. This recipe makes a slightly crunchy spread.

1 Carefully open the can of chickpeas. Put a colander in the (empty) sink, drain the chickpeas into the colander, then rinse them under the cold tap. Shake the colander well to drain off the water. Take out 1 heaped tablespoon of chickpeas and save to add at the end.

2 Tip the rest of the chickpeas into a food processor – ASK AN ADULT TO HELP whenever you use it. Add the tahini and olive oil.

3 Cut the lemon in half and squeeze out the juice with a lemon squeezer. Peel the garlic. Rinse the parsley. Put the lemon juice, garlic, parsley, salt, pepper and ground cumin in the food processor.

4 Run the processor for about 20 seconds, then turn it off. Scrape down the sides with a plastic spatula, then process again for about 10 seconds to make a fairly smooth purée. Add the saved whole chickpeas and process (using the pulse button if possible) for 3 to 4 seconds.

5 ASK AN ADULT to remove the sharp blade from the food processor. Spoon the hoummus into a serving dish and pat down the surface until it is smooth. Sprinkle the top with a little paprika, then serve.

6 The hoummus can be kept, well covered, in the refrigerator for up to 1 week.

Eat with tortilla chips (recipe below), spread on toast, or with raw vegetable sticks. Use a small serrated knife for cutting up the tomato. Ask an adult to help you if you haven't used a sharp knife before.

guacamole

1 large, very ripe avocado

1 large or 2 small tomatoes

1 lime

1 small garlic clove

a big pinch of salt

a big pinch of freshly ground black pepper

SERVES 2 TO 4

1 Using a small, sharp knife, cut the avocado in half all around from top to bottom. Twist the fruit gently and pull the two halves away from each other. Using a teaspoon, scoop out the flesh from each half into a small bowl, and throw away the stone and the skin. Gently mash the flesh with a fork to make a lumpy purée.

2 Rinse the tomato, then cut into quarters on a chopping board. Cut away the small green core at the top of the tomato, then chop each quarter into about 6 pieces. Add to the bowl. Cut the lime in half, then squeeze out the juice with a lemon squeezer. Add 2 teaspoons of the juice to the bowl, but keep the rest in case you need to add it later.

3 Peel the garlic and crush it with a garlic press or chop it very finely. Add to the bowl, then add the salt and pepper. Mix all the ingredients together with the fork – the mixture should be a bit lumpy. Taste and add more lime juice or salt and pepper as needed.

4 Eat immediately with these home-baked tortilla chips.

Turn ready-made soft wheat tortillas into a crunchy snack by baking them in the oven.

home-baked tortilla chips

4 large or 6 medium wheat flour tortillas

a large baking tray

SERVES 4 TO 6

1 ASK AN ADULT TO HELP YOU heat the oven to 160°C (325°F) Gas 3. Using kitchen scissors, cut each tortilla into 8 wedges. Spread the wedges in one layer, not overlapping, on the baking tray.

2 ASK AN ADULT TO HELP YOU bake them in the oven – they will need 15 minutes until they turn crisp and dry. Carefully remove the tray from the oven. Eat while still warm or let cool first.

With an adult to help with slicing, even quite small children can make this recipe. You'll need a blender, fresh unwaxed lemons, plus raspberries (or strawberries) for this fizzy, refreshing, healthy cool drink.

fresh raspberry lemonade

1 Rinse the lemons, because you will be using the skin as well as the juice.

2 Carefully cut each lemon into 8 with a small kitchen knife – ASK AN ADULT TO HELP YOU if you haven't used a kitchen knife before.

3 Put the lemons, sugar, raspberries and the 200 ml cold water in a blender. Make sure the lid is on tight, then blend for 10 seconds.

4 When the machine has stopped, remove the lid – check to see that the lemon pieces are about the size of peas. If there are still large pieces, blend again for 5 seconds. Remove the blender jug from the machine.

5 Put a medium sieve on top of a large serving jug. Carefully pour the lemon mixture into the jug through the sieve. Using a spoon, gently press down on the lemons in the sieve to squeeze out all the juice. Throw away the lemon pieces.

6 Top up the juice with the sparkling water – it will foam up, so add it slowly. Stir in the ice cubes and serve in chilled glasses.

2 large unwaxed lemons

75 g caster sugar

175 g fresh or frozen raspberries

200 ml cold water

500 ml sparkling mineral water

12 ice cubes

a blender

MAKES 4 GLASSES

Not a packet mix but the real thing – plain chocolate, milk and a dash of sugar, plus whipped cream and mini marshmallows if you really want to have fun.

real hot chocolate

1 Put the chocolate, sugar and milk in a small saucepan. ASK AN ADULT TO HELP YOU heat up the milk until it is almost boiling. Stir occasionally with a wooden spoon to help the chocolate melt.

2 Remove the saucepan from the heat and put onto a heatproof surface.

3 Using a rotary whisk, beat the milk until it is very smooth and foaming.

4 Carefully pour the hot chocolate into a mug and serve.

Other ideas
• Top with a swirl of cream (from a can, or whip some cream in a bowl with the rotary whisk). Sprinkle with a few mini marshmallows, then serve.

30 g plain chocolate

1 teaspoon caster sugar

200 ml milk

To serve (optional)

whipped cream

mini marshmallows

SERVES 1

Perfect on a really hot day when you want a filling drink, but not a milkshake. Ask an adult to help you if you haven't used a sharp knife before.

mango smoothie

1 ripe mango

1 ripe banana

250 ml chilled fresh orange juice

ice cubes

SERVES 2

1 Using a small sharp knife or a vegetable peeler, peel the mango over a plate to catch the drips. Carefully slice the yellow-orange flesh away from the large seed in the middle. Put all the slices and any juice into a large blender or food processor.

2 Peel off the banana skin, then slice up the banana and put the slices in the blender too. Pour in the orange juice. Put on the lid and secure tightly – ASK AN ADULT TO HELP YOU blend the mixture until completely smooth and foamy.

3 Pour into tall glasses and add ice cubes and a straw if you like.

Another idea
• If you chill the glasses in the refrigerator first (not the freezer) you get a lovely frosty effect.

This is a simple fruit and milk recipe – you can add a scoop of strawberry ice cream or sorbet if you like.

strawberry milkshake

250 g ripe strawberries

1 ripe banana

175 ml chilled milk

SERVES 2

1 Wipe the strawberries with kitchen paper, then carefully pull out the leafy green tops. ASK AN ADULT TO HELP YOU put the strawberries in the blender or food processor.

2 Peel the banana and cut it into slices. Put them into the blender, then add the cold milk.

3 Put on the lid and secure tightly – ASK AN ADULT TO HELP YOU blend the mixture until smooth and foaming.

4 Pour into chilled glasses and drink.

These are very popular in fancy ice cream parlours in New England. You can use your favourite kind of chocolate – milk, plain or white, or even layer them for a striped finish.

chocolate bananas

1 banana per person

30 g chocolate per banana

To decorate

chopped nuts or grated coconut

small bamboo skewers

SERVES 1

1 Peel the banana and cut it into pieces about 3 cm long. Carefully push a short skewer up through the centre of each piece. Wrap in clingfilm, then freeze for at least 2 hours or overnight.

2 When ready to eat, carefully and gently melt the chocolate in the microwave or in a small heatproof bowl set over a small saucepan of steaming hot water – ASK AN ADULT TO HELP YOU do this. It will take 15 seconds in the microwave or about 1 to 2 minutes over a saucepan.

3 Unwrap the banana pieces. Hold one piece by the stick over the bowl of chocolate, then spoon the chocolate over the banana to coat it.

4 The chocolate will set very quickly, so if you want to decorate it, sprinkle with chopped nuts or grated coconut as soon as you have coated the banana. You can add a second layer of chocolate in a contrasting colour.

5 Eat immediately.

400–650 ml fruit yoghurt, fromage frais or fresh fruit juice

a frozen lolly maker

MAKES 8 LOLLIES

You can buy plastic lolly-making kits quite cheaply at supermarkets and kitchen shops, and also by mail order. They usually make about 8 lollies at one time and fit easily onto a freezer shelf.

iced lollies

1 Each lolly will use 50 to 80 ml liquid. Using a teaspoon, carefully spoon the yoghurt into the lolly moulds, filling them almost to the top – the mixture will expand when it's frozen, so don't fill the moulds to the top. If using fruit juice, put it in a small jug and pour it carefully into the moulds.

2 Gently bang the moulds on the work surface 2 or 3 times to get rid of any large air bubbles (otherwise your frozen lollies will have holes in them).

3 Carefully push the handle tops into each lolly. Put the container into the freezer on a flat shelf – don't balance it on something else or you may end up with funny-shaped lollies. Freeze until solid – at least 4 hours or overnight.

4 To remove the lollies from the container, stand the container in a bowl of cold water (or hold it under the cold tap) for 1 to 2 minutes until the lollies lift out of the container.

Other ideas
• If you use fruit juice, shake the juice container carefully to mix the contents, then pour it into the lolly moulds and freeze as before.
• You can also freeze the recipes for Mango Smoothie and Strawberry Milkshake (page 25).

A quick snack is one thing, but this is real cooking. These recipes are fairly quick but need a bit of parental help with the dangerously hot bits. I've never met a child who doesn't like pasta, and simple fresh sauces are easily made. Daniel was given an inexpensive pasta machine for Christmas and when he has a friend round for supper, they would rather make their own pasta than watch television. It takes about 30 minutes for them to make pasta – for each portion allow 1 egg and 110 g Italian pasta flour (available from most supermarkets). Mix the dough in a processor, knead it, then cut in the machine following the manufacturer's instructions.

light suppers

This simple tomato sauce is perfect with pasta – and because there's no cooking, it's quick too.

fresh tomato sauce with pasta

400 g ripe tomatoes

a small bunch of fresh chives

a small handful of fresh basil leaves

1 garlic clove

4 tablespoons virgin olive oil

a pinch of salt

a pinch of freshly ground black pepper

To serve

300 g spaghetti

freshly grated Parmesan cheese

SERVES 4

1 Rinse the tomatoes and put them on a chopping board. Cut each tomato into quarters, then cut each quarter into about 4 chunks. Have a large heatproof serving bowl ready and put the cut tomatoes straight into the bowl. Using kitchen scissors, snip the chives into tiny lengths straight into the bowl. Tear the basil leaves and add to the bowl.

2 Peel the garlic and crush with a garlic press or chop finely and add to the bowl. Add the olive oil, salt and pepper. Stir thoroughly. Taste the sauce – it may need more salt and pepper, a pinch of sugar or even a squeeze of lemon juice, depending on the flavour of the tomatoes. Let the sauce stand while you cook the pasta – or for up to an hour – for the flavours to develop. If possible, cover the bowl and put it in the sun.

3 ASK AN ADULT TO HELP YOU cook the spaghetti in a large saucepan of boiling water with a pinch of salt. Let it cook for 8 to 10 minutes or follow the instructions on the packet. Drain carefully, then add the pasta to the sauce. Toss gently until well mixed, then serve with plenty of grated Parmesan cheese.

A simple and fast pasta dish that's good on its own or with cooked chicken (see Italian Roast Chicken page 87). While the pasta is cooking, you make the lemon and watercress dressing in the serving bowl.

zingy pasta

1 large unwaxed lemon

4 tablespoons single cream

15 g unsalted butter, at room temperature

75 g watercress sprigs, rinsed

3 big pinches of salt

freshly ground black pepper

250 g thin dried egg pasta, such as tagliolini

75 g freshly grated Parmesan cheese, to serve

SERVES 4

1 ASK AN ADULT to fill a large saucepan with water, add a pinch of salt, and set it over the heat to boil.

2 While the water is heating, rinse the lemon, then grate the yellow part of the skin into a large heatproof serving bowl – leave the white part on the fruit because it is bitter. You can grate with the fine-hole side of a grater or with a hand-held lemon zester which removes the zest in thin strips. Cut the lemon in half and squeeze out the juice with a lemon squeezer. Pour the juice into the serving bowl.

3 Add the cream, butter, watercress sprigs and remaining salt to the bowl, then add about 4 turns of the pepper grinder.

4 When the water boils, ASK AN ADULT TO HELP YOU add the pasta to the water and stir. Using a timer or clock, cook for 2 to 3 minutes or according to the packet instructions – pasta tastes best when it is not overcooked. ASK AN ADULT to drain the pasta and add it to the bowl. The heat of the pasta will warm the ingredients and wilt the watercress.

5 Hold a fork in each hand and carefully lift and toss the pasta several times so it is thoroughly coated in the sauce. Eat immediately sprinkled with Parmesan.

Strips of smoked salmon turn the creamy sauce for this pasta a pretty pink. For a stronger flavour, add snipped fresh chives or dill.

pink dolly's pasta

300 g egg fettuccine

150 g smoked salmon or smoked trout (trimmings are fine)

4 tablespoons crème fraîche or thick cream

black pepper

a small bunch of fresh chives or a few sprigs of dill

SERVES 4

1 To make the sauce, snip the smoked salmon into small strips (you don't have to do this with trimmings) and put in a small saucepan. Add the cream and about 3 grinds of pepper from the pepper mill.

2 ASK AN ADULT TO HELP YOU set the pan over the lowest possible heat and warm the ingredients so the cream melts and the salmon turns a pale pink. Turn off the heat under the pan.

3 Cook the pasta in boiling salted water following the recipe on the previous page. Allow 4 to 6 minutes' cooking time or follow the packet instructions.

4 When the pasta is just tender and ready to be drained, ASK AN ADULT to remove about half a ladle (about 50 ml) of water from the pasta pan and add it to the small pan with the sauce. Drain the pasta into a colander.

5 Tip the pasta into a large serving bowl and pour the sauce over the top. Hold a fork in each hand and carefully lift and toss the pasta until well mixed. Using kitchen scissors, snip the chives or dill straight onto the pasta. Then serve with salad or green vegetables.

Another idea
• Add 125 g frozen peas or sweetcorn to the sauce before you add the pepper.

This red, green and white salad is called Flag Salad because it is the same colours as the flag of Italy. Use your fingers to pull the mozzarella apart into stringy pieces, tear up the basil and salad leaves then scoop out the avocados with a teaspoon. Salad dressings are easy to make too – just put all the ingredients in a screw-top jar and shake them.

flag salad

1 Thoroughly wash the salad leaves in a bowl of cold water. Drain well, then spin-dry in a salad spinner or pat dry with kitchen paper. Tear any large leaves in half (discard any brown parts) and arrange on a large serving platter.

2 Wash the tomatoes. Very small cherry tomatoes can be left whole, but cut larger ones in half on a chopping board using a small serrated knife. Dot the tomatoes over the salad leaves.

3 Slice the avocados in half from top to bottom, then twist the avocados to separate the halves and pull apart. Use a teaspoon to scoop out the flesh in spoon-shaped pieces, straight onto the salad. Discard the big stones and skins.

4 Open the bags or containers of mozzarella over the sink and drain off the watery white liquid. Using your hands, pull the mozzarella into shreds and arrange on top of the salad. Rinse the basil leaves, then tear them up into big pieces and add to the salad.

5 To make the dressing, put all the dressing ingredients in a small screw-top jar. Fasten the lid securely, then shake the jar until the dressing looks creamy – this is called 'emulsified'. Open the jar, taste the dressing and add more salt or pepper as needed.

6 Pour the dressing in a thin stream over the top of the salad and eat it immediately.

75 g rocket leaves or watercress sprigs or 1 small lettuce

250 g cherry tomatoes

2 ripe avocados

2 balls mozzarella cheese, 150 g each

a handful of basil leaves

Dressing

2 tablespoons virgin olive oil

2 tablespoons balsamic vinegar

a big pinch of salt

a big pinch of freshly ground black pepper

¼ teaspoon honey

SERVES 4 AS A MAIN DISH: 6 AS A FIRST COURSE

You can make your own pizza from scratch in half an hour. You can add anything you like as a topping – though this mixture is always popular.

easy speedy pizza

1 ASK AN ADULT TO HELP YOU preheat the oven to 200°C (400°F) Gas 6. Grease 2 large baking trays with a little soft butter on a piece of kitchen paper.

2 Set a sieve over a large bowl. Tip the flour, sugar, bicarbonate of soda and salt into the sieve and sift into the bowl. Stir in the dried herbs.

3 With your hand, make a hollow in the middle of the flour and pour in the buttermilk or the yoghurt and milk mixture. Using one hand, start to mix the flour into the liquid, then gradually work all the flour into the dough to make a soft and slightly sticky mixture. If there are dry crumbs and it is hard to work all the flour into the dough, add 1 tablespoon of buttermilk or milk. However, if the dough is really sticky and feels very wet, work in more flour 1 tablespoon at a time.

4 When the dough comes together in a ball, tip it out of the bowl onto a work surface lightly sprinkled with flour. Work the ball of dough with both hands for 1 minute until it looks smooth.

5 Divide the dough into 4 equal pieces – use a round-bladed knife. Shape each piece into a neat ball. Flour your hands, then gently pat out each piece of the dough to a circle about 17 cm across. Set the circles slightly apart on the greased trays.

6 Wash your hands, then wipe down the work surface to make it easier to prepare the topping.

7 Open the can of tomatoes – ASK AN ADULT TO HELP YOU with this. Set a large sieve over a bowl, then tip the can of tomatoes into the sieve and leave them to drain for a couple of minutes.

Pizza base

450 g plain flour

1 teaspoon caster sugar

1 teaspoon bicarbonate of soda

1 teaspoon salt

½ teaspoon dried oregano or thyme

350 ml buttermilk OR 175 ml plain yoghurt plus 175 ml milk

butter, for greasing the pan

Cheese and tomato topping

400 g canned chopped tomatoes

1 tablespoon tomato purée

1 tablespoon olive oil

1 teaspoon dried oregano or thyme

a pinch of salt

a pinch of freshly ground black pepper

1 garlic clove

2 mozzarella cheeses, about 150 g each

Optional extras

green or black pitted olives, slices of pepperoni or ham, sliced red or green pepper or mushrooms

2 large baking trays, greased

MAKES 4 MEDIUM PIZZAS

8 Pour the tomatoes into a food processor or blender (the juice drained off can be saved for soups or sauces). Add the tomato purée, olive oil, herbs, salt and pepper to the processor. Peel the garlic and add it too. ASK AN ADULT TO HELP YOU blend the tomato mixture very briefly just to make a lumpy purée. Tip the mixture into a bowl.

9 Spoon 2 tablespoons of the tomato topping in the middle of each pizza. Spread the tomato mixture over the base leaving a 2 cm border of uncovered dough all around the edge.

10 Slice the mozzarella or pull it into long shreds. Arrange the pieces on top of the pizza.

11 Finally, top with as many extras as you like.

12 ASK AN ADULT TO HELP YOU bake the pizzas until they are light golden brown and bubbling – this takes about 15 to 18 minutes in the preheated oven.

13 Carefully remove from the oven, but let cool for a couple of minutes before eating – the melted cheese can burn your mouth.

Making a risotto is simple, but the special arborio rice does need constant stirring as it cooks. In the supermarket, it is sometimes called 'Italian risotto rice'.

pea and parmesan risotto

1 medium onion

2 garlic cloves

2 tablespoons virgin olive oil

300 g Italian arborio rice

120 g shelled fresh or frozen peas

about 750 ml hot vegetable stock

20 g unsalted butter

salt and freshly ground black pepper

100 g freshly grated Parmesan cheese

a few sprigs of parsley

SERVES 4

1 Peel the onion and garlic, then chop them finely – ASK AN ADULT TO HELP YOU do this in a processor or on a chopping board, using a small kitchen knife.

2 Put the olive oil in a medium, heavy-based pan.

3 Put the pan over very low heat and stir in the chopped vegetables. Cook gently for about 10 minutes so the onion turns clear and not brown. Stir in the rice (don't wash it first), then stir in the peas.

4 Turn up the heat to medium and add a ladle of the hot vegetable stock. Stir gently so it doesn't splash you, and as soon as the liquid is absorbed by the rice, add another ladle of stock.

5 Keep on stirring the rice very gently the whole time so it doesn't stick to the bottom or sides of the pan, and keep on adding the hot stock. It will take about 20 minutes of stirring before the rice is tender. Taste a few grains with a teaspoon, but let it cool first so you don't burn your mouth. The mixture should be creamy and moist, but not dry or very wet and soupy – the exact amount of stock you will need depends on the brand of rice you use and how fast the rice is cooking.

6 As soon as the rice is tender, turn off the heat. Add the butter, salt and pepper, plus half the grated cheese. Stir gently into the rice, then cover the pan and leave for 4 to 5 minutes.

7 Rinse the parsley sprigs and snip them with kitchen scissors. Uncover the pan, sprinkle the parsley on top, then serve immediately with the extra grated cheese.

No cooking needed here – slices of smoked salmon or smoked trout are arranged in chicory leaf 'boats', then topped with a tangy cream dressing. For a special meal, serve the boats with warm ready-made blini or wholemeal bread, such as the Grant Loaf (page 81). The palest chicory leaves will be the sweetest – don't choose green ones.

smoked salmon in chicory 'boats'

1 small crisp lettuce, or a bag of salad leaves

2 medium heads of chicory (total weight about 180 g)

125 g smoked salmon, smoked trout, ham or smoked turkey

Herb dressing

3 tablespoons crème fraîche

a squeeze of lemon juice

a big pinch of salt

a big pinch of freshly ground black pepper

a big pinch of cayenne pepper

1 tablespoon fresh dill leaves, parsley sprigs or a small bunch of chives

SERVES 4

1 Gently separate the lettuce leaves and wash them in plenty of cold water. Drain thoroughly in a colander, discard any brown or bruised leaves, then spin dry in a salad spinner or pat dry with kitchen paper.

2 Tear up any large leaves, then arrange the leaves on a large plate.

3 Using a small sharp knife, carefully cut off the stalk end of each head of chicory.

4 Gently peel off the leaves – take care not to tear them. Wash and dry the chicory leaves in the same way as the lettuce.

5 Choose the 16 largest and best leaves – save the rest to make another salad.

6 To make up the 'boats', set the chicory leaves, without overlapping, on top of the lettuce on the platter.

7 Using kitchen scissors, carefully cut the slices of smoked salmon or trout into 16 strips to fit inside the chicory 'boats'. Carefully arrange the fish in the chicory 'boats'.

8 To make the dressing, put the crème fraîche, lemon juice, salt, black pepper and cayenne pepper in a small bowl. Snip the fresh herbs into small pieces with kitchen scissors and add to the bowl. Stir gently, then taste – add more lemon juice, salt or pepper as needed.

9 Using a teaspoon, put a blob of the dressing in each chicory 'boat', then serve.

Sushi is a famous rice dish from Japan. There are many kinds, but one of the most delicious is a roll made of seaweed, rice and cucumber, then cut into bite-sized pieces. You dip them in soy sauce before eating. Another easy kind is made in an egg cup – just smoked salmon and rice, all wrapped up.

two kinds of sushi

400 ml Japanese sushi rice

Vinegar dressing

3 tablespoons Japanese rice vinegar

2½ tablespoons caster sugar

2 teaspoons salt

Hand vinegar

4 tablespoons Japanese rice vinegar

250 ml cold water

Egg cup sushi

125 g smoked salmon slices

Sushi rolls

1 medium cucumber, about 20 cm

3 sheets nori seaweed

To serve

Japanese soy sauce

pickled ginger (optional)

MAKES 10 EGG CUPS AND 36 ROLLS

Cooking the rice

1 To prepare the sushi rice, measure the rice in a measuring jug rather weighing it. Put a large bowl in the sink, add the rice, then cover with water from the cold tap. Swish your hand about in the water to wash the rice, then carefully tip off the water without tipping out any of the rice. Do this once more, then add enough cold water to cover the rice well, and let soak for 10 minutes.

2 Drain off the water, then drain the rice into a colander set over the sink.

3 Transfer the rice to a deep, heavy-based saucepan, and pour in 460 ml cold water. Cover the pan. ASK AN ADULT TO HELP YOU cook the rice. Bring the rice to a boil over high heat – this will take about 5 minutes.

4 Turn down the heat so it is quite low and let the water simmer without lifting the lid for 10 minutes, so that it's all absorbed. Turn off the heat and leave it, still without lifting the lid, for 10 to 15 minutes.

Making the vinegar dressing and hand vinegar

1 While the rice is cooking, make the vinegar dressing for the rice. Put the rice vinegar, sugar and salt in a small bowl, then stir well until dissolved.

2 To make the hand vinegar (which stops the rice sticking to your fingers), put the vinegar and water in a bowl and stir well.

Dressing the rice with vinegar

1 Take the lid off the cooked rice. ASK AN ADULT TO HELP YOU transfer the hot rice to a large shallow dish. Sprinkle with the vinegar dressing. Using a wooden spatula, fold the dressing into the rice – try not to stir, and ask someone to fan the air just above the rice as you do this to help the rice to cool quickly. Let cool for 5 to 10 minutes.

Making egg cup sushi

1 Using kitchen scissors, cut the smoked salmon slices into 10 to 12 pieces. *continued on next page*

sushi continued

2 Line the inside of one egg cup with a piece of clingfilm so it hangs over the edge of the cup.

3 Line the whole of the inside of the egg cup with a piece of smoked salmon, filling in any gaps with small trimmings.

4 Dip your hands in the hand vinegar (this stops the rice sticking to your fingers). Put about 1 tablespoon of the rice into the cup and press down gently with your thumbs. Try not to over-fill the egg cup. Fold any salmon hanging over the edge of the egg cup over the top of the rice. Lift the clingfilm up and out of the egg cup and put the moulded sushi upside down on a serving platter.

5 Repeat to make 10 pieces.

Making sushi rolls

1 Rinse the cucumber and put onto a chopping board. ASK AN ADULT TO HELP YOU cut off each end carefully with a sharp knife. Cut the cucumber in half lengthways and scoop out the seeds with a teaspoon to make 2 'boats'.

2 Cut each half cucumber lengthways into 3 strips. Cut each sheet of seaweed in half crossways (sometimes there is a line or crease to guide you).

3 Put the sushi mat (or you can use a sheet of clingfilm) on the work surface and put a half-sheet of seaweed on top.

4 Dip your fingers in the hand vinegar, take a handful of rice, 2 to 3 tablespoons, and pat it into a log shape. Then put the rice in the centre of the seaweed and flatten the rice with your fingers so it covers the seaweed leaving a 3 cm margin on the far side.

5 Put 1 strip of cucumber down the middle of the rice. Pick up the mat from the side closest to you and roll the mat over to meet the other side, keeping the cucumber in the centre as much as possible, and keeping the rice inside the seaweed, if using.

6 Lift the top edge of the mat, then press and roll the mat carefully so the join in the seaweed sticks together. Lift the roll off the mat and onto a board. Make 5 more rolls in the same way.

7 ASK AN ADULT TO HELP YOU cut each roll into 6 pieces. Arrange on a serving platter and serve with a dish of Japanese soy sauce for dipping, and pickled ginger slices.

Note Sushi shouldn't be put into the refrigerator because it makes the rice hard. If you are making it early for a party, keep the sushi in an airtight container in a very cool, well-shaded spot.

'Toad-in-the-Hole' is a funny name for little sausages cooked in Yorkshire pudding batter. Choose your favourite sausages – pork, beef, lamb, chicken or vegetarian. You will also need thick oven gloves, because the pan gets very hot. Younger children can mix the batter, but will need an adult to do the cooking.

toad-in-the-hole

1 ASK AN ADULT TO HELP YOU adjust the oven shelves – you will be using the middle one for the muffin tin, so make sure there is plenty of room for the batter to rise above the tin. Put a shelf under the middle one and put a large tray or roasting tin on it to catch any drips. ASK AN ADULT TO HELP YOU preheat the oven to 220°C (425°F) Gas 7.

2 To make the batter, put the flour, salt and pepper in a large bowl. Make a hollow in the centre, then break the eggs into the hollow. Pour the milk into the hollow.

3 Using a wire whisk, mix the eggs with the milk. Start to mix the flour into the hollow. When all the flour has been mixed in, whisk the batter well to get rid of any lumps.

4 Add the snipped chives and whisk them into the batter. (The batter can be made up to 3 hours before you start cooking.)

5 Using kitchen scissors, snip the links between the sausages. Wash your hands well after handling the sausages.

6 Put 1 teaspoon of oil into each hole of the muffin tin, then ASK AN ADULT TO HELP YOU put it into the oven to heat. Using thick oven gloves, remove the pan after 5 minutes – the oil will be very, very hot – and put it on a heatproof work surface. Carefully put 1 chipolata or half a large sausage in each hole, then ASK AN ADULT TO HELP YOU put the tin back in the oven for 5 minutes.

7 Pour or ladle the batter into a large jug and stir it once or twice.

8 Carefully remove the hot tin as before, then stand back (the oil can splutter) and carefully pour the batter into each hole so each one is half full. Gently replace the tin in the oven and bake for 20 minutes until golden brown and crispy.

9 Remove from the oven and ease each toad out of its hole with a round-bladed knife. Eat straight away with salad or green vegetables or even baked beans.

115 g plain flour

a pinch of salt

a pinch of pepper

2 large eggs

250 ml milk

a small bunch of fresh chives, snipped into 3 cm pieces with kitchen scissors

12 tiny chipolata sausages or cocktail sausages, or 6 larger sausages cut in half

4 tablespoons vegetable oil

a large tray or roasting tin

1 or 2 large muffin tins

thick oven gloves

MAKES 12 INDIVIDUAL TOADS: SERVES 4 TO 6

You can change this basic recipe using your favourite bits and pieces from the refrigerator. The main thing is to add plenty of vegetables – the omelette is basically vegetables stuck together with eggs and cheese – though you can also add strips of ham, pepperoni, or cooked bacon, chicken or turkey. This is easy!

spanish omelette

3 large eggs

1½ tablespoons cream (any kind)

2 tablespoons grated Cheddar cheese

a pinch of salt

a pinch of pepper

1½ tablespoons olive oil

Vegetables

2 spring onions

1 medium tomato

2 tablespoons peas (cooked or frozen)

2 tablespoons sweetcorn (cooked, frozen or canned)

½ red or green pepper, or courgette

1 cooked potato

SERVES 2

1 Break the eggs into a medium bowl. Add the cream, cheese, salt and pepper and mix well with a fork.

2 ASK AN ADULT TO HELP YOU put the olive oil in a non-stick frying pan and warm gently over low heat.

3 While the oil is heating, cut the spring onions into thin slices with a small, sharp knife, and cut the tomato into small chunks.

4 Add the onion, tomato, peas and corn to the oil and stir well with a wooden spoon. Cook gently for a few minutes while you slice the pepper or courgette, and cut the potato into small cubes the size of dice. Add all these to the pan and stir well.

5 Let cook for 2 minutes, then stir again and pour in the egg mix. Stir the whole mixture gently, then turn up the heat to medium and let cook until the eggs look almost set and no longer runny on the surface.

6 ASK AN ADULT TO HELP YOU remove the pan from the heat and slide the omelette out of the pan and onto a serving platter. Cut into wedges and eat.

This tomato soup is thickened with split red lentils and is packed with delicious ingredients. Serve with homemade bread, such as the Grant Loaf (page 81), for a filling meal.

tomato and red lentil soup

1 tablespoon virgin olive oil

1 medium red onion

1 medium carrot

1 celery stalk

1 garlic clove

400 g canned chopped tomatoes

1 tablespoon tomato purée

50 g split red lentils

400 ml vegetable stock

a big pinch of salt

a big pinch of freshly ground black pepper

a big pinch of sugar

2 tablespoons cream (any kind), to serve

SERVES 4 TO 6

1 Put the oil in a medium saucepan.

2 Peel the onion, peel the carrot with a vegetable peeler, wash the celery and peel the garlic. Using a small, sharp knife, trim off the ends of the onion, carrot and celery, then cut them all into chunks about 4 cm long. Put the onion, carrot, celery and garlic in a food processor. ASK AN ADULT TO HELP YOU process the vegetables until they are very finely chopped.

3 ASK AN ADULT TO HELP YOU put the saucepan on low heat to warm the oil gently. Carefully put the vegetables into the pan. Stir gently with a wooden spoon, then cover the pan with a lid and let cook very slowly for 5 minutes. Carefully lift the lid off the pan – the steam can burn you – and add the canned tomatoes, tomato purée, red lentils, stock, salt, pepper and sugar. Stir well, then turn up the heat so the mixture comes to the boil.

4 When the soup has boiled, cover the pan with the lid, then turn down the heat so that the soup simmers very gently. Let it cook for 30 minutes. While the soup is cooking, carefully lift the lid about every 10 minutes and stir the soup with a wooden spoon to stop the lentils sticking to the bottom of the pan and burning.

5 At the end of the cooking time, take off the lid, turn off the heat and let the soup cool for 5 minutes.

6 ASK AN ADULT TO HELP YOU ladle the soup into a blender or food processor and blend until smooth. You can also purée the soup in the saucepan with a hand blender, but take care not to splash yourself with the hot soup. If you have used a blender or processor, tip the soup back into the saucepan. Taste – add more salt, pepper or sugar as needed – then carefully warm up the soup over low heat (the thick soup can splutter as it comes to the boil, so stand back). As soon as it boils, turn off the heat, stir in the cream and serve.

This family favourite makes a good meal on a cold day. It is full of wonderful flavours – savoury, sweet, spicy and aromatic. Ask an adult to help you if you haven't used a sharp knife before.

sweet and spicy soup

1 medium onion

2 medium potatoes

50 g dried (ready-to-eat) apricots

100 g split red lentils

1 lemon

750 ml vegetable stock

¼ teaspoon ground cumin

a big pinch of salt

a big pinch of freshly ground black pepper

1 teaspoon virgin olive oil or a small piece of unsalted butter, to finish

SERVES 4 TO 6

1 Peel the onion, and then peel the potatoes with a vegetable peeler.

2 Using a small, sharp knife, cut the ends off the onion, then cut the onion, potatoes and apricots into chunks.

3 Put the onions, potatoes, apricots and lentils in a large, heavy-based saucepan.

4 Cut the lemon in half. Squeeze the juice from one half with a lemon squeezer (save the other half for later) and add to the pan. Pour in the stock, then add the cumin, salt and pepper. Mix well with a wooden spoon.

5 ASK AN ADULT TO HELP YOU put the pan over medium heat and bring to the boil. Carefully stir the pan, then cover it with the lid, turn down the heat to very low so that the soup simmers very gently and let it cook for 30 minutes. Very carefully lift off the lid and stir the pan every 10 minutes to stop the lentils from sticking to the bottom of the pan.

6 At the end of the cooking time, turn off the heat, lift off the lid and let the soup cool for 5 minutes

7 ASK AN ADULT TO HELP YOU ladle the soup carefully into a blender or food processor and blend until very smooth. The soup can also be puréed in the saucepan using a hand blender, but take care because the hot soup can burn if it splashes you.

8 Pour the soup back into the pan. Taste and add more lemon juice, salt, pepper or cumin as needed. Gently reheat the soup – be careful, because it can splutter as it comes to the boil. Turn off the heat and stir in the oil or butter and serve.

Note Any cold, leftover soup can be stored in an airtight container in the refrigerator for up to 4 days.

baking afternoon

This is where most children start to learn the pleasure of cooking – making gingerbread people, fairy cakes or a birthday cake for someone precious. No wonder this is what we remember with fondness; the afternoons spent squeezing doughs, cutting out shapes, pressing on colourful decorations, watching through the glass door of the oven as the aromas fill up the kitchen, then eating the results. There are recipes for the youngest children to play with, and more challenging ones for those keen to experiment with yeast doughs.

gingerbread people

350 g self-raising flour

a pinch of salt

1 tablespoon ground ginger

200 g caster sugar

115 g unsalted butter

85 g golden syrup

1 large egg

To decorate

raisins

edible silver balls

Mini-Smarties®

2 baking trays

shaped pastry cutters

**MAKES 14 FIGURES,
12 CM LONG**

Don't just make little people – look for cutters in the shape of a princess, a pony, teddy bear or Santa. Decorate them with chocolate chips, Mini-Smarties® or raisins.

1 ASK AN ADULT TO HELP YOU preheat the oven to 160°C (325°) Gas 3. Grease several baking trays with soft butter, using a piece of kitchen paper.

2 Set a sieve over a large bowl. Tip the flour, salt and ground ginger into the sieve and sift into the bowl. Add the sugar and mix in with a wooden spoon. Make a hollow in the centre of the flour.

3 Put the butter and syrup into a small saucepan. ASK AN ADULT TO HELP YOU melt the butter and syrup gently over very low heat – warm the pan just enough to melt the ingredients. Don't let the mixture become hot.

4 Carefully pour the melted mixture into the hollow in the flour.

5 Crack the egg into a small bowl and break up with a fork.

6 Pour the egg into the hollow on top of the melted mixture. Mix all the ingredients with a wooden spoon. As soon as the dough starts to come together, put your hands into the bowl and start to push the barely warm dough together. If the dough is too hot to handle, wait for it to cool.

7 As soon as the dough has come together into a ball, and is no longer crumbly, tip it out of the bowl and onto a work surface lightly dusted with flour.

8 With a rolling pin, gently roll out the dough to a large rectangle about 4 mm thick.

9 Cut out figures with your cutters, then transfer them carefully to the prepared baking trays with a fish slice or large spatula. Don't worry if their limbs or heads fall off – just press them back together again. Space the figures well apart, because they will spread in the oven. Gather all the trimmings into a ball, then roll out and cut more figures as before.

10 Decorate the figures with raisins, silver balls or Mini-Smarties®. ASK AN ADULT TO HELP YOU bake the figures – they will take about 15 minutes until golden brown. Watch them carefully, because they can quickly burn.

11 ASK AN ADULT TO HELP YOU carefully remove the trays from the oven and leave them on a heatproof work surface to cool for 5 minutes. This lets the soft biscuit mixture become hard. When the figures are firm, gently lift them onto a wire rack, using a large fish slice or spatula. Let them cool completely.

12 Store in an airtight container and eat within 1 week.

Everybody loves chocolate muffins! These are quick-mix and made with cocoa powder plus chocolate chips for maximum chocolate flavour.

double chocolate muffins

250 g plain flour

40 g cocoa powder

2 teaspoons baking powder

100 g caster sugar

80 g chocolate chips

2 large eggs

230 ml milk

125 ml sunflower oil

1 teaspoon pure vanilla essence

20 g chocolate chips, for sprinkling

a 12-hole deep muffin tin

paper muffin cases

a wire rack

MAKES 12

1 ASK AN ADULT TO HELP YOU preheat the oven to 200°C (400°F) Gas 6.

2 Put a paper muffin case in each hole of a 12-hole deep muffin tin.

3 Set a large sieve over a large bowl. Tip the flour, cocoa, baking powder and sugar into the sieve and sift into the bowl. Add the chocolate chips.

4 Break the eggs into a second bowl. Add the milk, oil and vanilla, then mix well with a fork. Add the flour mixture and gently stir with a wooden spoon.

5 Spoon the mixture into the paper cases – each one should be about half full. Carefully dot with chocolate chips.

6 ASK AN ADULT TO HELP YOU put the muffin tin into the hot oven. Cook them for about 20 minutes until well-risen and just firm. The chocolate chips become very hot, so take care not to touch them.

7 ASK AN ADULT TO HELP YOU to remove the tray carefully from the oven. Take the muffins out of the hot tin and put them on a wire rack to cool. This should take about 30 minutes.

8 These muffins are best eaten the same day.

This wonderfully fudgy cake is perfect for a birthday or any other party. Like all chocolate cakes, this one is best if you make it the day before you plan to eat it.

best-ever chocolate cake

100 g caster sugar

115 g unsalted butter, at room temperature, plus extra for greasing the cake tins

½ teaspoon vanilla essence

2 large eggs, at room temperature

230 ml soured cream, at room temperature

250 g plain flour

40 g cocoa powder

1 teaspoon baking powder

1 teaspoon bicarbonate of soda

a pinch of salt

Chocolate icing

175 g best-quality milk chocolate

90 g plain chocolate

230 ml soured cream

2 sandwich cake tins, 20 cm diameter

non-stick baking parchment or greaseproof paper

a wire rack

SERVES 8 TO 10

1 ASK AN ADULT TO HELP YOU preheat the oven to 180°C (350°F) Gas 4.

2 Grease the insides of the cake tins with a small amount of very soft butter on a piece of kitchen paper. Cut out 2 circles from a sheet of non-stick baking paper or greaseproof paper – put the cake tin on the paper and draw around it. Using scissors, cut inside the line so you have 2 circles the same size as the tins. Fit them into the bottom of each tin.

3 Put the sugar, soft butter and vanilla in a large bowl. Break the eggs into the bowl, then add the soured cream.

4 Set a large sieve over the bowl and tip the flour, cocoa powder, baking powder, bicarbonate of soda and salt into the sieve. Carefully sift these ingredients into the bowl.

5 Using a wooden spoon or electric hand mixer (use slow speed), beat the mixture for about 1 minute until smooth.

6 Spoon the mixture into the 2 tins so they are evenly filled, then spread the mixture so it is smooth.

7 ASK AN ADULT TO HELP YOU put the cakes in the oven. Bake them for 20 minutes, then carefully remove from the oven. Turn the cakes upside down onto the wire rack. The cakes will drop out, and you can peel off the lining paper and let them cool.

8 To make the icing, break up the chocolate bars and put into a heatproof bowl. ASK AN ADULT TO HELP YOU heat some water in a medium saucepan, then remove the pan from the heat as the water boils. Set the bowl over the pan of hot water and let the chocolate melt, stirring every minute.

9 When the chocolate has melted, carefully remove the bowl from the pan. Let the chocolate cool for 5 minutes, then gently stir in the soured cream to make a smooth, thick icing.

10 Set one of the cakes on a serving plate. Spread about one-third of the icing over the cake, then set the second cake gently on top of the first. Spread the rest of the icing on the top and sides of the cake to cover it completely. Leave in a cool spot until firm before you cut it – the cake is best if stored in an airtight container and cut the next day.

Unwaxed lemons are best if you can find them, because you need both the skin and juice for this simple but tangy loaf cake.

lemon drizzle loaf cake

175 g unsalted butter, very soft, plus extra for the tin

250 g caster sugar

2 unwaxed lemons

3 large eggs, at room temperature

250 g self–raising flour

½ teaspoon baking powder

115 ml milk, at room temperature

100 g caster sugar, to make the drizzle topping

a 900 g loaf tin

greaseproof paper or non-stick baking parchment

a wire rack

MAKES 1 LARGE CAKE

1 ASK AN ADULT TO HELP YOU preheat the oven to 180°C (350°F) Gas 4.

2 Lightly rub the inside of the loaf tin with a little soft butter. Cut a long strip of greaseproof paper or non-stick baking parchment the width of the tin. Press the paper into the tin so it covers the base and the 2 short sides. Trim off any excess paper. Cut some more paper and do the same for the long sides.

3 Put the soft butter and sugar in a large bowl.

4 Rinse the lemons, then grate the yellow zest straight into the bowl using a lemon zester or fine grater. Set the lemons aside.

5 Crack the eggs into the bowl.

6 Set a sieve over the bowl, put the flour and baking powder in it, then sift into the bowl. Add the milk, then beat with a wooden spoon or electric hand mixer (on low speed) for 1 minute until smooth and well mixed, with no streaks of flour.

7 Spoon the mixture into the prepared tin and spread the surface to make it smooth.

8 ASK AN ADULT TO HELP YOU put the tin into the heated oven. Bake the loaf for 50 to 55 minutes. To test if it is cooked, carefully remove it from the oven, then push a cocktail stick into the centre of the loaf. If the stick comes out clean, the loaf is ready. If it is sticky with mixture, then cook the loaf for another 5 minutes.

9 While the loaf is cooking, make the topping. Cut the lemons in half and squeeze out the juice with a lemon squeezer. Pour the juice into a small bowl. Add the sugar and stir for 1 minute to make a syrupy glaze.

10 When the loaf is cooked, carefully remove it from the oven and stand the tin on a wire cooling rack. Prick the top of the loaf all over with a cocktail stick to make lots of small holes in the loaf. Spoon the lemon syrup all over the top so it trickles into the holes in the loaf. Leave until completely cold before lifting the cake out of the tin. Peel off the lining paper and cut the loaf into thick slices.

11 Store in an airtight container and eat within 4 days.

Perfect for picnics and lunchboxes, and you can add your favourite nuts or dried fruit.

toffee loaf cake

250 g plain flour

1 teaspoon bicarbonate of soda

200 g light muscovado sugar

125 ml plain yoghurt

125 ml milk

1 large egg

20 g unsalted butter, plus extra for greasing

50 g chopped pecans, or mixed nuts or sultanas

a 450 g loaf tin

non-stick baking parchment or greaseproof paper

a wire rack

MAKES 1 MEDIUM CAKE

1 ASK AN ADULT TO HELP YOU preheat the oven to 180°C (350°F) Gas 4.

2 Lightly grease the tin with soft butter on a piece of kitchen paper, then cut a strip of greaseproof paper the width of the tin and about 36 cm long. Fit the paper into the base of the tin so it covers the 2 short sides.

3 Put the flour, bicarbonate of soda and sugar in a bowl.

4 Pour the yoghurt into a measuring jug, then top up with the milk (to make 250 ml). Break the egg into the jug, then mix the ingredients with a fork.

5 To melt the butter, ASK AN ADULT TO HELP. Either put it in a small saucepan over the lowest possible heat, or put it in a microwave-proof dish and microwave on MEDIUM for about 20 seconds, then pour into the jug.

6 Pour the liquids in the jug into the bowl. Mix well with a wooden spoon for 1 minute, then mix in the nuts or fruit.

7 Spoon the mixture into the tin. ASK AN ADULT TO HELP YOU put the tin into the hot oven. Bake for 45 to 50 minutes until golden brown. To test if the cake is cooked in the middle, push a cocktail stick into the centre of the cake, then gently pull it out. If the stick is clean, then the cake is cooked; if it is coated in cake mix, then cook for about 5 minutes more.

8 ASK AN ADULT TO HELP YOU remove the tin from the oven and put it on a wire rack to cool. Leave for 10 minutes, then lift the loaf out of the tin using the lining paper. Leave until cold on the wire rack. Serve in thick slices.

9 Store in an airtight container and eat within 4 days or freeze for up to 1 month.

These smell and taste wonderful. The recipe is traditional and simple, but the lemon zest makes it extra special. Eat the scones warm with butter.

lemon and thyme scones

1 ASK AN ADULT TO HELP YOU heat the oven to 220°C (425°F) Gas 7. Rub the baking tray with a little soft butter on a piece of kitchen paper.

2 Put the flour and sugar into a medium bowl.

3 Rinse the lemon under the cold tap, then dry with kitchen paper. Grate off the yellow zest with a lemon zester or the fine side of a kitchen grater. Put the lemon zest and thyme leaves into the bowl and mix all the ingredients well with your hand.

4 Using an ordinary table knife, cut the butter into tiny pieces and add to the bowl.

5 Toss the pieces of butter in the flour so they are well coated, then rub the butter into the flour – to do this, pick up a handful of the mixture with your fingers, then rub the mixture between the very ends of your fingers so the bits of butter become smaller and smaller as they mix with the flour. Keep rubbing in until the whole mixture looks like crumbs. Make a hollow in the centre of the crumby mixture.

6 Crack the egg into a measuring jug. Mix with a fork, just enough to break up the yolk and the white. Add enough milk to make up the mixture to 150 ml.

7 Pour three-quarters of the milk mixture into the hollow. Using the table knife, stir the liquid and flour mixture together to make a soft, coarse-looking dough. If the dough is dry and crumbly, and won't stick together, stir in more of the milk mixture, 1 tablespoon at a time.

8 Tip the dough out of the bowl and onto a work surface lightly covered with flour.

230 g self-raising flour

3 tablespoons caster sugar

1 unwaxed lemon

a big pinch of fresh thyme leaves

40 g unsalted butter, plus extra for the baking tray

1 large egg

about 100 ml milk

a baking tray

a round biscuit cutter, about 5 cm, or a drinking glass the same diameter

a wire rack

MAKES 8

9 Work and knead the ball of dough with your hands for a few seconds so it looks smoother. Dip your hands in a little more flour, then pat out the ball of dough until it is about 1.75 cm thick. Dip the biscuit cutter in flour, then cut out rounds. Gather up all the scraps of dough into a ball, then pat out again and cut more rounds.

10 Put all the rounds on the greased baking tray, arranging them slightly apart.

11 ASK AN ADULT TO HELP YOU put the tray into the hot oven, then bake for 10 to 12 minutes until golden brown.

12 AGAIN WITH ADULT HELP, carefully remove the tray from the oven and set it on a heatproof surface. Transfer the scones to a wire rack with a fish slice or metal spatula. Let cool until warm, then serve.

13 Best eaten the same day. They can also be toasted.

Another way

• You can also make scones in a food processor. Put the flour, sugar, lemon zest and thyme in the food processor. ASK AN ADULT TO HELP YOU blend for a few seconds just to mix the ingredients. Add the bits of butter to the bowl and blend again until the mixture looks like crumbs. Pour in three-quarters of the milk and egg mixture and process until the dough comes together in a ball, adding more of the milk mixture as needed. ASK AN ADULT to remove the blade carefully from the processor before you remove the dough. Pat out the dough and cut rounds as above.

Just a little spicy, these scones are good to eat
warm with soup or salad. An easy way to grate
cheese is to use a rotary grater, if you use a
kitchen grater, take care you don't grate your
fingers too – it's sharp.

cheese and chilli scones

230 g self-raising flour

a big pinch of salt

a big pinch of freshly ground
black pepper

a big pinch of crushed
chilli flakes

40 g unsalted butter, plus
extra for greasing the tray

60 g grated mature Cheddar
cheese

1 large egg

about 100 ml milk

2 tablespoons grated cheese,
for topping

a baking tray

MAKES 8

1 ASK AN ADULT TO HELP YOU heat the oven to 220°C (425°F) Gas 7. Put a little bit of butter on a piece of kitchen paper and rub it all over the baking tray. This is called 'greasing', and it will stop the scones from sticking to the tray.

2 Put the flour, salt, pepper and crushed chilli flakes in a large bowl and mix well. Using a round-bladed table knife, cut the butter into small pieces, then mix into the flour. Using the tips of your fingers, rub the butter into the flour so the mixture looks like crumbs.

3 Stir in the grated cheese, then make a hollow in the mixture.

4 Crack the egg into a measuring jug, then add enough milk to make up to 150 ml. Mix the egg into the milk with a fork, then pour three-quarters of this mixture into the hollow you've made in the bowl of flour.

5 Using a round-bladed table knife, stir the ingredients to make a soft but not too sticky dough. If the dough is stiff, dry and very crumbly, stir in more of the milk, 1 tablespoon at a time.

6 Lightly sprinkle a work surface with flour, then tip the dough onto it. Flour your hands and work the dough into a rough-looking ball. Flatten the ball to make a round about 18 cm across. With a round-bladed table knife, cut the dough into 8 wedges, like a cake. Brush the tops with a little of the leftover milk mixture or use a little extra plain milk. Sprinkle the cheese on the top.

7 Using a metal spatula, lift up the scones and put them on the prepared baking tray, spacing them slightly apart. They will expand in the oven and we don't want them to touch each other.

8 ASK AN ADULT TO HELP YOU put the tray into the preheated oven. Bake the scones for about 10 minutes until golden brown. WITH ADULT HELP, carefully remove the tray from the oven, transfer the scones to a wire rack and leave for a few minutes until just cool enough to eat. Eat with butter.

9 If there are any left over, you can toast them the next day.

It's not difficult to make bread. Not much can go wrong; you can kill the yeast (it's a living fungus believe it or not) with too much heat – if the mixing liquid is too hot for your little finger it's too hot for the yeast – but it can usually stand any amount of handling. This recipe gives you the method for a simple loaf, but you can also make animals, pizzas or a plait from the same dough. If you feel inspired, you can add fruit and nuts or cheese to the dough.

making bread

350 g unbleached white bread flour

1 teaspoon salt

10 g fresh yeast OR half a 7 g sachet easy-blend dried yeast

210 ml tepid water

butter, for greasing the tin

a 450 g loaf tin, lightly greased

MAKES 1 MEDIUM LOAF

1 Put the flour in a large mixing bowl. Add the salt (and the easy-blend dried yeast if you are using this), and mix everything with your hand. Make a hollow in the middle of the flour.

2 If you are using fresh yeast, put it in a small bowl and break it into small crumbs with your fingers. Add half the water and stir well with a teaspoon.

3 Pour the yeast liquid into the well, then the rest of the water. If you are using the dried yeast pour all the water straight into the well in the flour mixture.

4 Using your hand, slowly stir the flour into the liquid in the hollow – the mixture will turn from a thick batter to a soft dough as more flour is drawn in. Work the mixture with your hand until all the flour has been mixed in – flours vary from brand to brand, so if there are dry crumbs in the bowl and the dough feels very dry and hard to mix, add a little more water to the bowl, 1 tablespoon at a time. If the dough is very sticky and sticks to your fingers or the sides of the bowl, add more flour 1 tablespoon at a time.

5 Sprinkle a little flour over the work surface and tip the dough out of the bowl onto it. Using both hands, knead the dough by stretching it out away from you then gathering it back into a ball again. Turn the ball around and stretch the dough out again then gather it back into a ball. Keep doing this for about 10 minutes – it's hard work but you can take a short rest every now and then. You can also knead the dough in a large food mixer with the dough hook attachment – it will take 4 minutes on very low speed, ASK AN ADULT TO HELP you do this.

6 Put the kneaded dough back into the mixing bowl – it now has to be left to rise. Yeast dough likes to be kept warm and moist, so cover the bowl with a snap-on lid, or put the bowl into a large, clean plastic bag (supermarket carriers work well) and tie it closed.

continued on next page

making bread continued

7 If you leave the bowl near a warm stove or above a radiator, it will take about 1 hour to double in size. At normal room temperature it will take 1½ to 2 hours, depending on the time of year. If it's in a cool unheated room, it will 2 to 6 hours, or you can leave it overnight in the refrigerator.

8 While the dough is rising, put some butter on kitchen paper and rub it lightly over the inside of the loaf tin. This is called 'greasing'.

9 When the dough has doubled in size, uncover the bowl and gently punch down the dough with your fist. Sprinkle your work surface lightly with flour, then tip the dough onto it. Shape the dough into a brick to fit your tin. Lift the dough into the tin and gently press it in.

10 Put the tin in a plastic bag again, and let the dough rise in a warm place until doubled in size – about 1 hour.

11 While the dough is rising, ASK AN ADULT TO HELP YOU preheat the oven to 220°C (425°F) Gas 7.

12 Uncover the risen dough and ASK AN ADULT TO HELP YOU put the tin in the oven. Bake it for 30 minutes until a good golden brown. AGAIN WITH ADULT HELP, carefully remove from the oven and tip the bread out of the tin onto a wire rack to cool.

13 To make sure the bread is cooked right through, carefully tap the underside of the loaf with the back of your hand – it should sound hollow like a drum, if you hear a dull 'thump', then put the loaf, without the tin, back in the oven for another 5 minutes, then test again.

14 Let the bread cool on the wire rack before cutting.

15 Best eaten within 5 days or frozen for up to 1 month.

other breads

The same dough can be made into rolls – when it comes to the shaping part, divide the dough into 8 even pieces. Roll into balls, or sausage shapes, or make into animal shapes with raisin eyes (crocodiles, mice, cats, pigs, snakes, hedgehogs with spikes made by cutting the dough with kitchen scissors), or flatten the balls to make baps. Let rise, spaced well apart on 2 greased baking trays, then bake in the preheated oven for 15 to 20 minutes, depending on the thickness of the rolls.

To make pizza bases – add 1 teaspoon dried thyme or oregano to the flour at the same time as the salt, then add 1 tablespoon good olive oil to the water when mixing the dough. When it comes to shaping the dough, divide it into 4 even pieces, then shape each piece into a ball. Flatten each ball to a round about 17 cm across. Put the pizza bases on 2 baking trays, spaced well apart. Let rise for about 20 minutes while you prepare the topping (see the recipe on page 40).

To make a plaited loaf – mix the dough with tepid milk instead of water. When it comes to shaping the dough, divide the dough into 3 equal pieces. Using your hands, roll the dough into 3 sausage shapes about 40 cm long. Pinch the 3 strands together at one end, then plait the dough, pinch the other ends together and tuck underneath. Carefully lift onto a greased baking tray, then let rise and bake as in the main recipe.

To make shiny bread – just before baking the bread, dip a pastry brush into a little beaten egg or milk and carefully brush over the top of the dough, but don't let it drip onto the tin or the tray or the dough will be 'glued' on, and be difficult to remove after baking. If the dough is glazed in this way, you can sprinkle it with sesame seeds, poppy seeds, sunflower seeds or grated cheese and they will stick to the dough.

To make cheese bread – add 100 g grated Cheddar cheese to the flour at the same time as the salt.

My son Dan started making this wonderful golden bread when he was six. It's a great recipe for new bakers – the dough can be kneaded in an electric mixer using a dough hook, and it only needs one rising in the tin – so no shaping needed! It's done in stages, so read the whole recipe before you start. Eat the bread thickly sliced, with or without butter, or toasted for breakfast or at tea time. (It's called Cornish bread because saffron used to be grown in Cornwall.)

cornish bread

½ teaspoon saffron strands

300 ml milk

500 g unbleached white bread flour

1 teaspoon salt

150 g unsalted butter, plus extra for greasing the loaf tin

50 g light muscovado sugar

15 g fresh yeast or a 7 g sachet easy-blend dried yeast

100 g mixed dried fruit (sultanas, raisins and currants)

a 450 g loaf tin (about 18 x 12 x 7 cm), greased with butter and gently warmed

MAKES 1 MEDIUM LOAF

1 Pick up the strands of saffron and rub them between your fingers into a heatproof jug. ASK AN ADULT TO HELP YOU heat the milk in a small saucepan or in the microwave for 2 minutes on HIGH until it is very hot but not boiling. Carefully pour the milk onto the saffron, then cover the jug with a saucer or small plate and leave to infuse (this means to let the milk absorb the flavour and colour of the saffron) for 2 to 4 hours. You don't have to stay while this happens.

2 Put the flour and salt in a bowl or the bowl of an electric mixer. If you are using easy-blend dried yeast, add it now. Mix the flour and salt with your hand. Cut the butter into small pieces with a round-bladed table knife and put them in the bowl. Toss the pieces of butter in the flour so they are coated with it, then pick up a handful of the mix and rub it between your fingers so it falls back into the bowl. This is quite a sticky business, but after about 5 minutes the lumps of butter will have been crushed and mixed with the flour. Keep rubbing the butter into the flour until the mixture looks like breadcrumbs. Mix in the sugar.

3 ASK AN ADULT to warm up the milk gently – it should just feel comfortable to touch.

4 If you are using fresh yeast, crumble it between your fingers into the milk and stir well.

5 With your hands, make a hollow in the middle of the flour mixture, then pour in the warm saffron milk. Mix with your hands until you have a heavy sticky dough.

6 Sprinkle your work surface with flour, then lift the dough out of the bowl onto the work surface. Knead the dough, stretching it out, then gathering it back into a ball. Do this for 5 minutes, though you can take a rest now and again. At the end, the dough will feel much more elastic and springy. Alternatively, if you have a large electric mixer, knead the dough using the dough hook attachment for 4 to 5 minutes on the lowest speed – ASK AN ADULT FOR HELP in setting this up.

7 When you have finished kneading, sprinkle the fruit onto the dough. Mix it in with your hands by squeezing the dough through your fingers.

8 Lift the dough into the warm tin, pressing it down well to squeeze out the air bubbles.

9 Put the tin into a large plastic bag and gently inflate the bag to make a tent, so the plastic doesn't touch the dough. Tie the ends closed, then leave in a warm place until the dough has risen to the top of the tin – about 1 hour. Meanwhile ASK AN ADULT TO HELP YOU preheat the oven to 180°C (350°F) Gas 4.

10 Remove the loaf from the plastic tent and ASK AN ADULT TO HELP YOU put the loaf in the oven. Bake it for about 1 hour until a good golden brown. Again, WITH ADULT HELP, remove the loaf from the oven and tip it upside down on the wire rack. Tap the underside of the loaf with the back of your knuckles – if there is a hollow drum-like sound, the loaf is cooked. If there is a heavy, dull thump, put the loaf back in the oven for another 5 minutes.

11 Let cool completely before slicing. Best eaten within 4 days or freeze for up to 1 month.

The best recipe for your first-ever loaf – we call it 'Honey I'm wholemeal!' It was invented accidentally by Doris Grant about 60 years ago and proves that sometimes accidents taste good. Unlike most bread doughs, this one is not kneaded or shaped and has only one rising – in the tin. The Grant Loaf makes great sandwiches and toast, and is lovely with cheese or soup. Tip: with bread making it's a good idea to use cold water for cleaning up (otherwise you'll get wallpaper glue).

the grant loaf

700 g organic stoneground wholemeal bread flour

1 teaspoon salt

15 g fresh yeast or a 7 g sachet of easy-blend dried yeast

1 tablespoon honey

600 ml tepid water

butter, for greasing

a 900 g loaf tin, greased with butter

MAKES 1 LARGE LOAF

1 Put the flour and salt in a large bowl (stand the bowl on a damp towel to stop it wobbling) and mix well with your hand. If using dried yeast, mix it in now.

2 Put the fresh yeast in a small bowl and crumble it with your fingers. Put the honey in the bowl and about 125 ml of the warm water. Mix with a teaspoon until smooth.

3 Use your hand to make a hollow in the centre of the flour. Pour the yeast liquid into the hollow, then the rest of the water. Leave for 5 minutes – the yeast liquid will become very bubbly. If using dried yeast, add the honey and water and continue with the recipe.

4 Mix the flour into the liquid with your hand, then mix well for 1 minute, moving the dough from the sides of the bowl into the centre. Mix 1 more minute until the dough feels very slippery and elastic and comes cleanly away from the sides of the bowl.

5 Lift the dough into the tin and smooth the surface with a plastic spatula. Cover loosely with a clean, damp tea towel. Leave in a warm spot for 30 to 40 minutes or until the dough rises to within 1 cm of the top of the tin. While the dough is rising, ASK AN ADULT TO HELP YOU heat the oven to 200°C (400°F) Gas 6.

6 ASK AN ADULT TO HELP YOU put the loaf tin into the oven. Bake it for about 35 to 40 minutes.

7 To test if the loaf is cooked, ASK AN ADULT TO HELP YOU remove the tin from the oven. Using oven gloves or a thick oven-cloth to protect your hands, remove the loaf from the tin and tap it underneath. If it sounds hollow, like a drum, then the loaf is cooked. If it sounds like a dead thump, then return it to the oven for another 5 minutes.

8 Transfer the loaf to a wire rack until cold.

9 Best eaten within 4 days or freeze for up to 1 month.

Another idea
• Add 1 or 2 tablespoons sunflower seeds or pumpkin seeds to the dough when you add the salt.

We always seem to have extra bodies to feed at weekends, so everyone helps with Saturday dinner and Sunday lunch, from planning menus, to shopping, setting the table, cooking, then finally serving to a round of applause (don't mention the washing up). Each child has a special menu – for Stevie it's always Bang Bang Chicken, made exactly as they do in her favourite Chinese restaurant. Dan likes to enjoy a roast lunch on Sunday, so he makes Italian chicken legs with roast vegetables, followed by meringues. Emily is still hooked on pancakes with maple syrup. It's a really fun way to spend time together as a family.

a proper meal

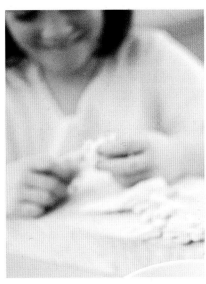

This is a favourite cold salad from our local Chinese restaurant – ready-cooked smoked or 'plain-roast' chicken is arranged on sticks of cucumber then topped with a creamy peanut butter dressing.

bang bang chicken

400 g ready-cooked boneless chicken, such as smoked chicken, cold roast chicken or cold turkey

1 medium cucumber

1 large carrot

salad leaves such as crispy lettuce or Chinese leaves, about 75 g

Bang bang dressing

5 tablespoons crunchy peanut butter

1 spring onion

1 teaspoon sesame oil

1 teaspoon soy sauce

1 teaspoon caster sugar

1 teaspoon Chinese white rice vinegar or cider vinegar

1 teaspoon rice wine or water

3 tablespoons hot water

SERVES 4

1 Remove any skin from the chicken and discard. Pull or cut the chicken into shreds the size of your little finger, then put onto a plate.

2 Rinse the cucumber. Cut off the ends and discard. Cut the cucumber in half lengthways, then in half crossways. Cut each piece into lengthways slices the width of your little finger. Put on another plate.

3 Peel off the carrot skin with a vegetable peeler, then cut off the ends and discard.

4 Make carrot ribbons by 'peeling' the carrot with the peeler to make ultra-thin long strips of carrot.

5 Rinse the salad leaves and dry thoroughly in a salad spinner or pat dry with kitchen paper. Tear any large leaves into bite-sized pieces. Arrange the leaves on a serving dish. Scatter the cucumber sticks and carrot ribbons over the leaves. Lastly, arrange the chicken on the top.

6 To make the dressing, put the peanut butter in a small bowl. Rinse the spring onion. Using a small knife, cut off the hairy root end and the very dark leaves at the top. Cut the spring onion into very thin slices and add to the peanut butter. Add the sesame oil, soy sauce, sugar, vinegar, rice wine or water and hot water to the bowl. Stir gently until well mixed. Taste the dressing – it should be a harmonious balance of salty, sweet and sour flavours, so add more vinegar, sugar or soy as you think is needed. The dressing should be just thin enough to spoon over the chicken, so if it is too thick stir in another tablespoon or so of hot water.

7 When the sauce seems perfect, spoon it over the chicken and serve.

It's hard to resist the smell of roasting chicken and, because this dish uses chicken pieces, there's no difficult carving, and the gravy appears during cooking. Choose organic chicken legs if you're hungry, otherwise large thighs, because these have the most flavour and it's fun to chew the meat off the bones. Serve with Roasties (page 94) or pasta and a green vegetable or Flag Salad (page 39).

italian roast chicken

4 chicken legs or thighs

4 unpeeled garlic cloves

1 large lemon

2 tablespoons olive oil

sea salt and freshly ground black pepper

4 large sprigs fresh thyme or rosemary

1 or 2 ovenproof baking dishes, big enough to hold the chicken in one layer

SERVES 4

1 ASK AN ADULT TO HELP YOU preheat the oven to 220°C (425°F) Gas 6.

2 While the oven heats, get the chicken ready for roasting; you will need ovenproof baking dishes that can also be the serving dishes.

3 Put the chicken pieces straight from the bag they came in into the dishes, skin side facing up, and check that the pieces don't overlap each other. When you've done this wash your hands thoroughly with soap and hot water. Make sure anything touched by the raw chicken is also thoroughly washed; this is important to avoid the spread of bacteria which could make you ill.

4 Put the garlic cloves in the dishes between the chicken pieces. Cut the lemon in half and squeeze out the juice with a lemon squeezer. Pour the juice over the chicken, then pour the oil over the top so the skin is evenly coated in liquid. Sprinkle with 4 pinches of salt and then about 3 turns of the pepper grinder. Finally, set a sprig of thyme or rosemary on the top of each piece of chicken.

5 ASK AN ADULT to put the baking dishes into the heated oven. Set the timer for 40 minutes for large legs, and 35 minutes for thighs. As the chicken cooks, the legs become a crispy golden brown, surrounded by a light brown cooking-juice gravy.

6 ASK AN ADULT to remove the dishes from the hot oven and put onto the table.

thai meatballs with chicken

Mildly spicy and full of flavour, these chicken balls are made with your hands, then simply baked in the oven – no frying needed. Serve with Thai fragrant rice and extra sweet chilli sauce (it's mild, not hot – a bit like Thai tomato ketchup) for dipping.

50 g fresh bread (about 2 medium slices)

500 g minced chicken or turkey

1 egg

2 spring onions

½ teaspoon ground coriander

a small bunch of fresh coriander leaves, about 15 g

1 teaspoon fish sauce or soy sauce

2 teaspoons sweet chilli sauce, plus extra for serving

vegetable oil, for greasing the dish

a large baking dish

MAKES 12: SERVES 4

1 ASK AN ADULT TO HELP YOU preheat the oven to 200°C (400°F) Gas 6.

2 Tear up the bread and put it into a blender or processor. ASK AN ADULT TO HELP YOU process the bread until it turns into crumbs. Tip the crumbs into a bowl. Add the minced chicken or turkey. Crack the egg into the bowl. Wash your hands well after touching raw meat or eggs.

3 Rinse the spring onions. Using a small knife, cut off the hairy root ends and the very dark leaves at the top. Cut the onions into very thin slices. Add to the bowl, then add the ground coriander. Using kitchen scissors, snip the fresh coriander leaves straight into the bowl. Add the fish sauce or soy sauce and the sweet chilli sauce to the bowl. Mix well with your hands then roll the mixture into small balls – use about 1 tablespoon of mixture for each.

4 Rub the base of a large baking dish with oil, then arrange the balls in the dish. ASK AN ADULT TO HELP YOU put it into the preheated oven to bake for 25 minutes until golden brown and cooked all the way through.

5 While the meatballs are cooking, wash your hands well, then make the rice (right).

6 Serve the meatballs straight from the baking dish with the rice and extra sweet chilli sauce in a small dish for dipping.

thai fragrant rice

250 g Thai fragrant rice

a pinch of salt

ENOUGH FOR 4

1 ASK AN ADULT TO HELP with this recipe because it involves boiling water.

2 Fill a large saucepan half full with water and put it on the stove. Cover with a lid, then turn on the heat and leave until the water boils (about 5 to 10 minutes).

3 Carefully pour the rice into the water, add the salt and stir gently. When the water starts to boil again, turn the heat down so the water doesn't bubble over the sides of the pan. Leave to boil gently (this is called simmering) for 10 minutes. Alternatively, follow the directions on the packet.

4 Make sure the sink is empty, then set a colander in the middle. ASK AN ADULT to pour the saucepan rice into the colander. Shake the colander well to drain off all the water, then tip the rice into a serving bowl and serve straight away with the Thai chicken meatballs.

salmon filo parcels

4 pieces skinless salmon fillet,
about 125 g each

40 g unsalted butter, at room
temperature

2 small or 1 large piece of stem ginger,
about 25 g

sea salt and freshly ground black pepper

200 g filo pastry, thawed if necessary

1 lemon, to serve

vegetable oil, for greasing the dish

a large ovenproof baking dish

MAKES 4

Filo pastry is easy to use. You don't have to mix it or roll it out – just don't uncover it until the last moment or it will get very dry. In this recipe, boneless, skinless pieces of salmon are topped with a gingery butter (made with stem ginger preserved in syrup) then wrapped up in pastry and baked.

1 ASK AN ADULT TO HELP YOU preheat the oven to 190°C (375°F) Gas 5.

2 Lightly grease the baking dish or roasting tin with a little vegetable oil on a piece of kitchen paper.

3 Rinse the 4 pieces of salmon under the cold tap, then pat dry with kitchen paper.

4 Put the butter in a small bowl and stir with a teaspoon until soft. Lift the ginger out of the syrup and put it on a small plate. Using a small knife, cut the ginger into thin slices. then cut the slices into strips. Add the ginger to the butter, then add the salt and pepper and mix well. Divide the mixture into 4 equal pieces.

5 Unwrap the filo pastry and separate and count the sheets. You will need an equal number for each parcel. Brands of filo vary from shop to shop, and each brand has different sized sheets, but arrange the sheets to make 4 rectangles, about 30 x 25 cm by overlapping or folding the sheets. If you have to cut sheets in half, use kitchen scissors.

6 Put a piece of fish right in the middle of each rectangle. Spread the top of each piece of fish with a portion of the butter. Fold the pastry over the fish as if you were wrapping up a Christmas parcel, then fold the ends underneath. Arrange the parcels in the prepared dish, then ASK AN ADULT TO HELP YOU put the dish in the oven.

7 Bake in the preheated oven for 25 minutes until golden brown. ASK AN ADULT TO HELP YOU take the dish out of the oven.

8 Serve the parcels hot on 4 plates, together with the lemon cut into 4 wedges.

beef rendang

Not all curry is mouth-stingingly hot. This is a gentle, aromatic, meat curry from Indonesia made all in one pot, with diced beef. Tamarind purée is sold in small jars from supermarkets or Asian stores. Serve with Thai fragrant rice (page 89) and green beans.

500 g diced braising steak

1 tablespoon tamarind purée

1 cinnamon stick

1 tablespoon dark muscovado sugar

2 tablespoons soy sauce

250 ml unsalted beef or vegetable stock

¼ teaspoon ground black pepper

¼ teaspoon freshly grated nutmeg

6 green cardamom pods

2 medium red onions

3 garlic cloves

3 cm piece of fresh ginger

SERVES 4

1 Put the meat in a heavy medium saucepan or casserole dish. Add the tamarind, cinnamon stick, sugar, soy sauce, stock, pepper and nutmeg.

2 Crush the cardamom pods with a mortar and pestle (or with the end of a rolling pin). Throw away the green husks and keep the tiny black seeds. Crush the seeds and add to the pan.

3 Peel the onions, garlic and ginger. Cut each onion in 4 and cut the ginger into thick slices. Put the onions, garlic and ginger in a food processor or blender and ASK AN ADULT TO HELP YOU blend the mixture until it is very finely chopped, almost a coarse purée.

4 Spoon this mixture into a saucepan. Stir gently until well mixed.

5 Set the pan over medium heat and bring the mixture to the boil. ASK AN ADULT TO HELP YOU stir gently and carefully, then cover the pan with a lid and turn down the heat to very low so the mixture bubbles very gently.

6 Let cook for 1½ hours, stirring now and then. You don't have to stay all the time it's cooking. In fact, you could ask an adult to do the stirring. Finally, remove the lid and cook uncovered for 20 to 30 minutes until the sauce is very thick. Remove the cinnamon stick and serve.

It's hard to imagine a roast dinner without crunchy roast potatoes, not to mention roast parsnips, roast sweet potatoes and more. So here is an easy way to cook all your favourite vegetables in one roasting pan.

roasties

500 g baking potatoes

500 g parsnips

500 g sweet potatoes

500 g large carrots

3 tablespoons virgin olive oil

a big pinch of sea salt

several grinds of black pepper

3 sprigs of thyme or
rosemary (or both)

a large roasting tin

SERVES 4 TO 6

1 ASK AN ADULT TO HELP YOU preheat the oven to 220°C (425°F) Gas 7 (the oven may already be on if you are cooking chicken or meat).

2 Peel all the vegetables with a vegetable peeler. Using a medium sharp knife, cut off the ends of the parsnips and carrots, then carefully cut all the vegetables into similar-sized chunks. They shouldn't be too neat and even, but aim for chunks about 4 cm long.

3 Put all the vegetables in a large roasting tin. Pour the oil over the top, sprinkle with the salt and pepper, then add the herbs, pushing them between the vegetables.

4 Using both hands, toss the vegetables in the oil and seasonings so they are very well mixed. Spread out the vegetables so they are in a single layer.

5 ASK AN ADULT TO HELP YOU put the vegetables into the hot oven. Cook for about 1 hour, but every 15 minutes during the cooking time, ASK AN ADULT TO HELP YOU remove the tray carefully from the oven and gently turn over the vegetables so they cook and brown evenly (the cut surface next to the metal tray cooks quickest).

6 At the end of the cooking time, ASK AN ADULT TO HELP YOU remove the tray carefully from the oven. Transfer the roasties to a serving dish, removing any twiggy bits of the herbs. Serve immediately.

corn-on-the-cob

For each ear of corn you will need:

25 g unsalted butter

a little salt and freshly ground black pepper

*an ovenproof dish big enough
to fit the corn in a single layer*

metal cooking tongs

SERVES 1

Corn is nicest eaten as soon as possible after picking. You don't always have to cook it in boiling water. Barbecuing is good, but roasting in the oven is just wonderful. How many can you eat?

1 ASK AN ADULT TO HELP YOU preheat the oven to 200°C (400°F) Gas 6.

2 If the corn still has its green leafy covering, it must be shucked – pull off the leaves from the pointy top end, then pull off all the silky hairs.

3 To melt the butter, ASK AN ADULT TO HELP. Either put it in a small saucepan over the lowest possible heat, or put it in a microwave-proof dish and microwave on MEDIUM for about 20 seconds.

4 Pour the melted butter into the baking dish and add a big pinch of salt and pepper for each ear of corn. Put the corn into the dish then rotate them in the butter mix so they are well coated.

5 ASK AN ADULT TO HELP YOU cook the corn in the heated oven – this will take 30 minutes. ASK AN ADULT TO HELP YOU turn the corn over twice carefully during this time – metal cooking tongs are the best thing to use.

6 The corn will be very lightly browned, and too hot to eat immediately, so let them cool for 5 to 10 minutes after they come out of the oven.

Also known as 'fruit salad on a stick'. You can use your favourite fruits for these brochettes, as long as you can thread them onto bamboo skewers. Choose a good mix of colours and textures like kiwifruit, bananas, strawberries, peaches, or different kinds of melon, depending on what's in season. Use this as a guide.

fresh fruit brochettes

2 kiwifruit

1 large or 2 small bananas

1 peach or nectarine

16 strawberries

8 bamboo skewers

SERVES 4

1 Peel the kiwifruit with a vegetable peeler.

2 Put them on a clean board and carefully cut in half with a small sharp knife.

3 Turn the fruit cut side down onto the board, then cut each half into 4 wedges.

4 Peel the banana(s) and cut into a total of 8 chunks.

5 Rinse the peach or nectarine under a cold tap. Slice in half from top to bottom, then twist to separate the halves. Ease out the seed, then turn the halves cut side down on the board and slice each half into 4 wedges.

6 Wipe the strawberries with a soft cloth. You can pull out the green leafy tops if you like.

7 Carefully thread the fruit onto the skewers starting and finishing up with a strawberry so each skewer has 2 strawberries, a wedge each of kiwifruit and peach and a chunk of banana.

8 Eat carefully so the juice doesn't drip down your chin.

When my niece was 10 she had a 'cooking' birthday party sleepover. She chose pizza and these pretty tarts, and each guest made her own dinner. The pastry base is a rich shortbread, and the topping consists of small fresh strawberries brushed with hot jelly to make a glossy professional glaze. Younger children will need adult help with baking.

little strawberry tarts

Tart base	Strawberry topping
230 g plain flour	**about 500 g small fresh strawberries**
70 g icing sugar	
170 g unsalted butter, straight from refrigerator	**about 230 g redcurrant or raspberry jelly**
2 large egg yolks	*2 or 3 baking trays*
½ teaspoon pure vanilla essence	*a pastry brush*
a little butter, for greasing	**MAKES 4 TO 6**

1 Put the flour and icing sugar into a large sieve set over a bowl and sift to remove any lumps. Tip the mixture into a food processor. Cut the cold butter into small cubes and add to the flour and icing sugar. ASK AN ADULT TO HELP YOU turn on the processor and blend the mixture until there are no large lumps and it looks like fine breadcrumbs. Add the 2 egg yolks and vanilla. Blend the processor again until the dough sticks together in a ball shape. ASK AN ADULT TO HELP YOU remove the dough from the processor (the blade is dangerous), then wrap the dough in clingfilm or greaseproof paper and chill in the refrigerator for 30 minutes.

2 The dough can make 4 large or 6 smaller individual tarts, so divide it into 4 or 6 equal pieces as needed. Put a little bit of butter on a piece of kitchen paper and rub it all over the baking trays to grease them.

3 Roll each piece of dough into a ball with your hands, then put on the baking trays, setting them well apart (they will spread in the oven). With your fingers, press and pat out the dough to make circles about 7 mm thick. You will have either 4 circles, 11 cm across, or 6 circles, 10 cm across. Pinch the edges with your fingertips to make a pretty shape, then prick the bases all over with a fork (the tiny air holes will stop the base bubbling up in the oven). Chill in the refrigerator for 10 minutes.

4 Meanwhile, ASK AN ADULT TO HELP YOU preheat the oven to 180°C (350°F) Gas 4.

5 ASK AN ADULT TO HELP YOU bake the circles for 20 minutes until they are a light golden colour. Carefully remove the trays from the oven and let the circles cool on the trays.

6 Check the strawberries and discard any bruised ones. Rinse in a colander and pat dry with kitchen paper. Remove the green stems and leaves with your fingers or with a small knife.

7 Spoon the jelly into a small saucepan. Add 1 tablespoon of water and ASK AN ADULT TO HELP YOU heat it very gently, stirring with a wooden spoon. The solid jelly will melt and become a thick, smooth, hot syrup. Remove from the heat before it starts to boil.

8 Set each cooked pastry circle on a serving plate. Using a pastry brush, brush a little hot jelly over each circle. Arrange the strawberries on the base with their pointy ends up. Brush the berries with the hot glaze to coat them completely. If the glaze starts to set before you've finished, gently warm it again.

9 Leave until set – about 20 minutes – before serving. Best eaten the same day.

1 ASK AN ADULT TO HELP YOU preheat the oven to 120°C (250°F) Gas ½.

2 Cut out 2 rectangles of non-stick baking parchment to fit the 2 baking trays, then set one on each tray.

3 Put the egg whites and cream of tartar in a large, spotlessly clean and grease-free bowl (grease will make it difficult to whisk the whites). Stand the bowl on a damp cloth to keep it from wobbling.

4 Using a rotary or electric hand mixer, start whisking the egg whites. Whisk steadily until the whites turn into a stiff white foam – lift out the whisk and there will be a little peak of white standing on the end.

5 Mix the sugar with the cinnamon, then whisk it into the egg whites, 1 tablespoon at a time, to make a stiff, glossy, golden meringue.

6 Scoop 1 heaped teaspoon of the mixture out of the bowl, then use a second teaspoon to help you push the meringue onto the prepared tray to make a craggy mountain-like heap. Scoop out the rest of the mixture in the same way to make about 16 heaps, spaced slightly apart on the trays.

7 ASK AN ADULT TO HELP YOU put the baking trays into the hot oven. Bake for 2 hours. Carefully remove the trays from the oven and let cool. Peel the meringues off the lining paper and pile them up in a serving bowl. The meringues can also be stored in an airtight container for up to 1 week.

8 To make the fruit salad using fresh fruit, rinse the blueberries in a colander under the cold tap. Drain thoroughly, then tip into a serving bowl. Add the raspberries, rinse the strawberries and pull out the green leafy tops. Put two-thirds of the strawberries in the bowl with the other berries. Put the rest of the strawberries in a small bowl, add the sugar and mash the berries with a fork to make a coarse, juicy purée. Tip this mixture into the bowl of berries and stir gently until just mixed. Cover and leave at room temperature until ready to serve, up to 2 hours.

9 If you are making the salad with frozen fruit, put all the frozen berries and the sugar in a serving bowl. Mix gently, then cover and set aside to defrost slowly, 2 to 4 hours.

10 Serve the meringues and fruit salad with vanilla ice cream.

You'll need a rotary whisk or electric hand mixer to beat the egg whites to a stiff snow. Serve the crunchy meringues with a mixture of fresh red berries in summer, or frozen ones in winter.

cinnamon meringues with fresh fruit

Meringues

2 egg whites

a pinch of cream of tartar (optional)

110 g caster sugar

¼ teaspoon ground cinnamon

non-stick baking parchment

2 baking trays

Fruit salad

125 g blueberries

125 g raspberries

250 g small strawberries

1 tablespoon icing sugar

vanilla ice cream, to serve

SERVES 4 TO 6

Lovely at any time of year, this pudding is a combination of juicy fruits and a crunchy topping. Eat warm or cold with ice cream or yoghurt.

juicy fruit crisp

2 large Granny Smith apples, or
2 peaches, or 2 medium pears

250 g fresh or frozen (don't thaw)
raspberries, blueberries or blackberries

2 tablespoons caster or demerara sugar

Crisp topping

125 g plain flour

80 g demerara sugar

90 g unsalted butter, plus extra for greasing the dish

a medium ovenproof baking dish

SERVES 4

1 ASK AN ADULT TO HELP YOU preheat the oven to 190°C (375°F) Gas 5.

2 Lightly grease the baking dish by rubbing a little butter over the base and sides.

3 Peel the apples or pears (there is no need to peel peaches) with a vegetable peeler. Cut out the core with an apple corer or by cutting the fruit into quarters, then cutting out the core with a small knife. Cut the peaches in half, then twist to separate the halves, the seed may come out easily, if not cut the peach away from the seed. Discard the skin and cores, then cut the apples, pears or peaches into chunks the size of half your thumb.

4 Put the fruit in the dish, then add the berries. Sprinkle with the sugar and toss gently until just mixed. Spread the fruit evenly in the dish.

5 To make the topping, put the flour and sugar in a mixing bowl. Cut the butter into small pieces and add to the bowl. Using your hands, squeeze the mixture together until it becomes all soft and sticky and there are pea-sized lumps of dough. Sprinkle this mixture over the fruit – don't press it down.

6 ASK AN ADULT TO HELP YOU put the dish into the oven. Let it bake for 25 minutes until bubbling and golden on top.

7 ASK AN ADULT TO HELP YOU remove the dish carefully from the oven. Eat the crisp hot, warm or cold.

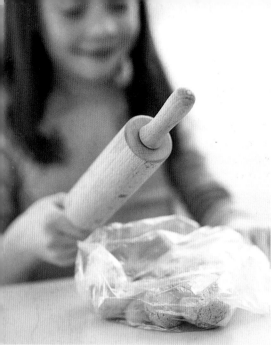

Ready-made filo pastry works well here, and it doesn't matter what it looks like when it goes into the oven. When it's baked and dusted with icing sugar, your strudel will taste and look sensational. Choose slightly tart, well-flavoured apples.

apple strudel

200 g filo pastry

9 amaretti biscuits (50 g)

4 medium apples (800 g)

70 g caster sugar

1½ teaspoons ground cinnamon

50 g unsalted butter, plus extra for greasing

2 tablespoons slivered almonds or raisins or dried blueberries

icing sugar, for dusting

a large baking tray

SERVES 6

1 ASK AN ADULT TO HELP YOU preheat the oven to 200°C (400°F) Gas 6. Rub the baking tray with a little soft butter.

2 If the pastry is frozen, let it defrost before using. Do not unwrap the pastry until you are ready to use it, because it will dry out and become crumbly.

3 Put the amaretti biscuits into a plastic bag and tap carefully with a rolling pin until the biscuits have turned into crumbs.

4 Peel the apples with a vegetable peeler, then cut out the cores with an apple corer and cut in four, or cut the apples in quarters then cut out the cores with a small sharp knife. Cut each quarter into 4 slices. Put all the apple slices in a large bowl.

5 Mix the sugar and cinnamon in another bowl.

6 To melt the butter, ASK AN ADULT TO HELP. Either put it in a small saucepan over the lowest possible heat, or put it in a microwave-proof dish and microwave on MEDIUM for about 25 seconds.

7 Unwrap the pastry and separate the sheets. Overlap the sheets to make a rectangle about 55 x 70 cm. Using a pastry brush, lightly brush about half the melted butter over the pastry. Sprinkle the amaretti crumbs on top, then add the apple slices leaving a clear border of about 5 cm all around the edges. Sprinkle with the sugar and cinnamon mixture, then add the almonds or dried fruit.

8 To roll up the strudel, first fold over the pastry borders along the two short sides, then fold over the pastry border along one long side. Roll up the strudel from this side, and don't worry if the pastry splits and the filling falls out, just push it all back together with your hands. You will need an extra pair of hands and a couple of spatulas to help you transfer the roll to the buttered baking tray. If the roll is too big for the size of your tray you may have to curve the roll into a horseshoe shape. Again press it all back together. Brush all over with the rest of the melted butter.

9 ASK AN ADULT TO HELP YOU put the strudel into the oven. Bake it for 35 minutes, or until golden brown.

10 ASK AN ADULT TO HELP YOU remove the tray carefully from the oven, then dust icing sugar over the top of the strudel. To do this, you can use a sugar shaker filled with icing sugar, or put 2 tablespoons of icing sugar in a small sieve and sift over the top of the strudel.

11 Cut into thick slices and eat warm or at room temperature with cream or yoghurt.

A great mix-and-bake recipe with white chocolate lumps for those who don't or can't eat nuts. For a special birthday meal, serve the brownies warm with vanilla ice cream or the warm fudge sauce below (also great with bananas and ice cream).

brownies and ice cream

140 g unsalted butter

4 large eggs

320 g caster sugar

1 teaspoon pure vanilla essence

75 g cocoa powder

140 g plain flour

100 g best-quality white chocolate

vanilla ice cream, to serve

kitchen foil

a 20 cm square cake tin

MAKES 16

1 ASK AN ADULT TO HELP YOU preheat the oven to 160°C (325°F) Gas 3.

2 While the oven heats up, cut kitchen foil into a square with sides about 25 cm, then press the foil into the square cake tin to line the base and the sides.

3 To melt the butter, ASK AN ADULT TO HELP. Either put it in a small saucepan over the lowest possible heat, or put it in a microwave-proof dish and microwave on MEDIUM for about 40 seconds.

4 Crack the eggs into a large mixing bowl. Tip the sugar into the bowl, then add the vanilla. Stir well with a wooden spoon for 1 minute until completely mixed.

5 Pour in the melted butter and stir for another 1 minute.

6 Set a large sieve over the mixing bowl and sift the cocoa and flour onto the egg mixture. Stir well for another 1 minute, getting right down to the bottom of the bowl. When there are no streaks of flour, break up the white chocolate bar into small chunks and add to the bowl. Stir until just mixed, then spoon the mixture into the foil-lined tin.

7 ASK AN ADULT TO HELP YOU bake the brownies – they will take about 40 minutes in the centre of the oven. To test if the brownies are ready, push a cocktail stick into the mixture about half way between the sides and the centre. Pull out the stick – if it is clean, then the brownies are ready, if the stick is sticky, then cook for 5 minutes more.

8 Leave the tin to cool on a wire rack. When completely cold, remove the brownies from the tin, peel off the foil, then cut into 16 squares.

9 Store in an airtight container and eat within 5 days or freeze for up to 1 month.

warm fudge sauce

140 g plain chocolate

30 g unsalted butter

2 tablespoons golden syrup

100 ml creamy milk or single cream

SERVES 6

1 Break up the chocolate into chunks and put in a small saucepan. Add the butter, golden syrup and milk or cream. ASK AN ADULT TO HELP YOU put the pan on the lowest possible heat. When the butter and chocolate start to melt, stir gently every minute or so to make a smooth sauce. When the sauce is hot, ASK AN ADULT TO HELP YOU take the pan off the stove and carefully pour the sauce into a serving jug.

2 Serve the sauce with the brownies. If there is any leftover sauce, let it cool, then cover and store in the refrigerator ready for next time.

This is where lots of people start cooking – first mixing the batter, then graduating to whisking egg whites (a rotary or electric hand mixer is a big help), folding the two together, then finally to cooking and flipping. The youngest child is usually 'pancake monitor' and is in charge of carrying each batch of just-cooked pancakes to the table.

1 To cook the pancakes, you will need a large, heavy frying pan (non-stick or cast iron if possible), or a flat griddle, or electric frying pan. If it isn't non-stick, rub the inside with a little oil.

2 ASK AN ADULT TO HELP YOU preheat the pan on the lowest setting while you make the batter. When you cook the pancakes, you should increase the heat up to medium-to-low.

3 To make the pancakes, put the flour, salt and sugar in large bowl and mix well with a wire whisk. Make a hollow in the centre of the flour.

4 Have another bowl ready for the egg whites. To separate the egg whites from the egg yolks, crack one of the eggs on the rim of the bowl so the shell is broken around the middle. Hold the egg over the empty bowl. Put both thumbs into this crack and gently pull the 2 halves of the shell away from each other so the clear egg white falls into the bowl and the round yellow yolk is left in one of the shells – this is not easy to do at first, so if the yolk falls into the bowl, lift it out with a spoon. Put the yolk into the hollow in the flour in the other bowl. Repeat with the other egg.

5 Pour the milk into the hollow in the flour on top of the yolks. Using the wire whisk, mix the milk and yolks together, then – a little at a time – stir in some of the flour. The liquid will become quite thick, and you may have to give it a good whisk to get rid of the lumps.

6 To melt the butter, ASK AN ADULT TO HELP. Either put it in a small saucepan over the lowest possible heat, or put it in a microwave-proof dish and microwave on MEDIUM for about 20 seconds. Pour the melted butter into the batter and whisk until you can't see it.

american pancakes with blueberries

a little oil, for greasing

120 g plain flour

a big pinch of salt

1 tablespoon caster sugar

2 large eggs

150 ml milk

25 g unsalted butter

175 g fresh or frozen blueberries

To serve

maple syrup

peanut butter

MAKES 12: SERVES 4

7 Using a rotary whisk or electric hand mixer, whisk the egg whites until they are very stiff and white – stiff enough not to fall out of the bowl if you turn it upside down (we test this over Grandpa's head – luckily he's bald).

8 Spoon the whites into the other bowl and gently stir the two mixtures with a large metal spoon. Try to use a 'cut downwards and turn over' movement with the spoon instead of mixing round and round – this is called 'folding'. It is better to have small lumps of white than a completely smooth batter.

9 WITH AN ADULT TO HELP YOU, start cooking the pancakes. Turn up the heat under the pan to medium/low.

Add a large spoonful of batter to one side of the pan – it will spread out to about 10 cm across. Drop about 6 blueberries into the centre of the pancake – it will still be liquid. After about 1 minute, check to see if small bubbles are breaking on the surface of the pancake and it has begun to set. Using a spatula or palette knife, lift the pancake up just above the pan, then flip it back over into the pan to cook the other side. This may be messy to begin with, but they will always taste good. Cook the pancake for another minute, then lift out of the frying pan. Cook the rest of the mixture in the same way (try cooking 2 or 3 at once). Eat straight from the pan with any leftover blueberries and maple syrup or even spread with peanut butter.

lunchboxes

Lunch doesn't need to be the same boring things day after day. Explain to your kids that they don't have to eat the same food as everyone else – they can make themselves a special lunch. Start with sandwiches. Most people have cheese or ham (peanut butter is outlawed by many schools), but look at the different kinds of bread on sale in bakeries and supermarkets. How about a bagel or ciabatta roll? If they usually go for cheese spread explore what else is on the cheese counter – Emmental has big holes and is quite mild: mozzarella is not just used in pizzas. If they like ham, try a mild salami or smoked turkey for a change (staff at the deli counter usually let you taste before you buy).

sandwiches

Everyone loves sandwiches, and we all have our favourite fillings. I've listed some of the lovely breads available, and just a few filling or spread ideas here. Mix and match them, or make up your own ideas.

Sliced bread and rolls Try making your own bread from the recipes in this book (pages 75 to 81), as well as buying interesting varieties from the supermarket bread counter, or from special bakers' shops. Our favourite filling is
• Tuna mayo – drain a 200 g can of tuna, then put the tuna in a small bowl. Stir in 2 tablespoons of mayonnaise and some ground black pepper. Cut a 5 cm piece of cucumber in half lengthways, then cut both halves into very thin slices. Stir into the tuna. It can be kept in the refrigerator for 4 days. This mixture can also be used to fill tomatoes (cut off the tops then scrape out the seeds with a teaspoon) or the hollow in celery stalks.

Pita bread comes in white, wholemeal and flavoured (with coriander or red pepper for example). Split them open at one end, then open out to make a pocket.
• Peel a carrot, cut off the ends, then grate the rest. Mix it with hoummus (page 16) and fill (add some salad leaves too).
• Take 2 tablespoons of canned cannellini beans, drain, then mash with a fork, stir into guacamole (page 19) and fill the pita bread.
• Fill with some bought taramasalata, then add thin slices of cucumber or lettuce leaf.

Bagels are sold white or wholemeal, plain or topped with seeds or onion flakes (there are also flavoured bagels and sweet bagels). Slice in half carefully (take extra care if using a bagel slicer).
• Spread with cream cheese (plain or flavoured with herbs) or cottage cheese. Add slices of tomato or smoked salmon, and cucumber.

Croissants can be large or small, plain or cheese-flavoured. Carefully slice in half (they can fall apart), then fill. Because croissants are so buttery, they don't need spreading with butter.
• Fill with a slice of mild Swiss cheese and a slice of ham.
• Or a slice of cheese and some good strawberry jam.

Wraps can also be large or small, made from wheat flour tortillas, plain or flavoured, or from other flatbreads such as Indian village bread, or Egyptian lavash. Choose an easy-to-eat filling, such as sliced chicken or turkey with watercress or maybe guacamole. Spread the filling over the base, then roll it up tightly and wrap in clingfilm to hold it together in your lunchbox.

Small shell or 'bow-tie' pasta works best. The dressing is a tangy lemon and olive oil, and you could use cooked sweetcorn instead of the olives.

tuna pasta salad

60 g small pasta shapes

2 tablespoons pitted black or green olives or 2 tablespoons cooked sweetcorn

5 cm piece of cucumber

5 cherry tomatoes

200 g canned tuna

a few fresh chives

Olive oil dressing

2 tablespoons olive oil

1 tablespoon lemon juice

½ teaspoon Dijon or mild mustard

a pinch of salt

a pinch of freshly ground black pepper

MAKES ENOUGH FOR 2 MEALS

1 ASK AN ADULT TO HELP YOU cook the pasta. Fill a medium saucepan two-thirds full with cold water, then bring to the boil. Add the pasta, stir gently, then let boil until tender – about 8 minutes (or follow the directions on the packet).

2 Put a colander into the empty sink and ASK AN ADULT TO HELP YOU by straining the pasta into the colander. Rinse the pasta in the colander, under the cold tap, so it cools quickly and rinses off the starch. Drain thoroughly in the colander while you make the rest of the salad.

3 Put the olives in a bowl.

4 Cut the cucumber into about 6 thick slices, then cut each slice into quarters. Add to the bowl. Cut the tomatoes in half, and add.

5 Open the can of tuna with a can opener, then carefully drain off the liquid. The lid will be sharp, so remove it carefully. Tip the tuna into the bowl and break the lumps into small flakes with a fork. Using kitchen scissors, snip the chives into small pieces and add to the bowl.

6 Put all the ingredients for the dressing into a screw-topped jar, and screw on the lid. Shake well, then open the jar and taste the dressing – you may want to add a little more salt or pepper.

7 Pour the dressing over the salad, then mix everything very gently with a metal spoon. Cover tightly and store in the refrigerator for up to 48 hours.

Couscous is a kind of pasta (not a grain) and it doesn't need cooking. You just add boiling water and let it soak for a little while. It makes a filling salad, but needs plenty of crunchy vegetables for colour and texture.

couscous salad

125 g couscous

1 tablespoon olive oil

a big pinch of salt

a big pinch of dried oregano or thyme

2 spring onions

1 medium carrot

6 cherry tomatoes

80 g sugar snap peas, green beans or mangetout

2 eggs

Dressing

2 tablespoons olive oil

1 tablespoon lemon juice

a big pinch of salt

a big pinch of freshly ground black pepper

SERVES 2

1 ASK AN ADULT TO HELP YOU to prepare the couscous. Bring water to the boil in a kettle. Put the couscous in a heatproof bowl, then add 200 ml boiling water (or follow the instructions on the packet). Add the oil, salt and dried herbs, then gently stir with a spoon. Cover the bowl with a saucepan lid, tray, plate or even a clean tea towel and leave for 5 minutes for the couscous to swell and soften.

2 Uncover the bowl, stir gently with a spoon and let cool. While the couscous cools, prepare the rest of the salad.

3 First, use a small sharp knife to cut the spring onions into thin rings.

4 Peel the carrot with a vegetable peeler, then cut off the ends with a small sharp knife. Make carrot ribbons with the vegetable peeler by peeling off long, thin lengths of carrot. Cut each tomato in half. Cut off the very ends of the sugar snap peas, green beans or mangetout.

5 ASK AN ADULT TO HELP YOU cook the vegetables – half fill a saucepan with cold water, bring to the boil over high heat, carefully add the carrot strips and the sugar snaps, beans or mangetout, then cook for 3 minutes so they are still crunchy. Put a colander in the sink and ASK AN ADULT to strain the vegetables into the colander. Rinse under the cold tap to stop the vegetables cooking any more, then leave to drain really well.

6 To cook the eggs, put them in a small saucepan. Add cold water to the pan so the eggs are just covered. Put the pan over medium-low heat and set the timer for 12 minutes. When the timer bell rings, ASK AN ADULT to remove the pan from the heat and put it in the sink. Turn on the cold tap and let it run over the eggs for 1 minute to cool them. Pour off the water, then gently tap the eggs on the work surface to crack the shells so you can peel them off. If small bits of shell stick to the eggs, rinse them under the cold tap. Cut the eggs into quarters.

7 To make the dressing, put all the ingredients into a screw-top jar, put the lid on tightly and shake well.

8 Add all the ingredients, including the dressing, to the cold couscous and gently mix the salad. Taste it, then add more salt, pepper or lemon juice as needed. Cover the bowl tightly with clingfilm and store in the refrigerator for up to 48 hours.

Other ideas
• Instead of the hard-boiled eggs, use cold cooked chicken (about 100 g) torn into shreds.
• If your school allows you to eat nuts at lunch, you can add a couple of tablespoons of toasted cashew nuts.

These jam-filled cookies are sturdy enough to survive life in a lunchbox, and are fun to make. You can use raspberry or any other flavour jam. They will keep for a week in an airtight container.

gran's raspberry buns

1 ASK AN ADULT TO HELP YOU preheat the oven to 200°C (400°F) Gas 6.

2 Rub the baking trays with a little soft butter on a piece of kitchen paper. This will prevent the buns from sticking to the baking tray.

3 Put the flour and sugar in a bowl and mix well with your hand.

4 Cut the butter into tiny pieces with a round-bladed knife and add to the bowl.

5 Toss the pieces of butter in the flour so they are well coated, then start to rub the pieces of butter into the flour – to do this, pick up a handful of the mixture with your fingers, then rub the mixture between the very ends of your fingers so the bits of butter become smaller and smaller as they mix with the flour. Keep rubbing in until the whole mixture looks like breadcrumbs.

6 Make a hollow in the centre of the crumby mixture.

7 Break the egg into a small bowl, add the milk and mix with a fork.

8 Tip the egg mixture into the hollow, then stir both mixtures together with a round-bladed knife to make a soft dough. If the dough is too dry and the crumbs won't stick together, add extra milk, 1 tablespoon at a time. If the dough is too wet and sticky, add 1 tablespoon extra flour until it is right.

9 Divide the dough into 16 even pieces. Roll each piece into a ball with your hands and set the balls well apart on the baking trays.

10 Stick your finger in the middle of each ball to make a small hole (don't go right down to the bottom).

11 Using a teaspoon, put a pea-sized amount of the jam into the hole, then pinch the dough back together to cover the hole (don't worry if it looks a bit messy at this point).

12 ASK AN ADULT TO HELP YOU bake the cookies. Cook for 10 minutes at 200°C (400°F) Gas 6, then turn down the heat to 180°C (350°F) Gas 4 and cook for 5 minutes more. Carefully remove the baking trays from the oven, sprinkle the buns with a little sugar and let cool for 5 minutes (the jam becomes incredibly hot in the oven and can easily burn you).

13 Using a fish slice, transfer to a wire cooling rack and let cool completely.

225 g self-raising flour

90 g caster sugar, plus extra for sprinkling

110 g unsalted butter from the refrigerator, plus extra for greasing the trays

1 large egg

1 tablespoon milk

about 1 tablespoon raspberry jam

2 baking trays

MAKES 16

Porridge oats and crunchy seeds mixed with golden syrup make a sweet end to lunch. Wrapped in foil, the flapjacks stand up to life in a lunchbox, and the oats will give you energy all afternoon. If you are not keen on seeds, use raisins or chopped nuts instead – they're all good.

crunchy oat flapjacks

1 ASK AN ADULT TO HELP YOU preheat the oven to 200°C (400°F) Gas 6. While the oven is heating up, rub the baking tin with a little soft butter on a piece of kitchen paper. This will prevent the flapjacks from sticking to the tin.

2 Measure the oats, flour, sugar, pumpkin seeds, sunflower seeds and sesame seeds into a large bowl. Mix well with a wooden spoon.

3 Put the butter and golden syrup into a small saucepan, and ASK AN ADULT to put it on the lowest heat on top of the stove until just melted.

4 Pour the melted butter and syrup into the bowl with the oats and stir well.

5 Tip the oat mixture into the tin and spread it evenly with the wooden spoon. Lightly press it down so it all sticks together while it cooks.

6 ASK AN ADULT to put the tin in the oven and take it out after 20 minutes when it should look light golden brown. Stand the tin on a heatproof surface and, without touching the hot tin, gently cut the mixture into 9 squares (2 cuts each way).

7 Let cool then remove from the tin.

8 Store in an airtight container and eat within 1 week.

100 g porridge oats

3 tablespoons self-raising flour

3 tablespoons caster sugar

1 tablespoon pumpkin seeds or raisins

1 tablespoon sunflower seeds or chopped nuts

1 tablespoon sesame seeds

100 g unsalted butter, plus extra for greasing the tin

1 tablespoon golden syrup

a cake tin, 18 cm square

MAKES 9

Stevie fell in love with this heavenly soup one hot day at a Shaker restaurant in New England. It needs very ripe and juicy fruit. It is quick and easy to make in a blender and keeps well overnight in the refrigerator. Pour into a vacuum flask, add an ice cube, then enjoy it after a hot morning in class.

cool strawberry soup

500 g ripe strawberries

250 g plain yoghurt

1 tablespoon clear honey, or to taste

4 fresh mint or basil leaves

a pinch of salt and freshly ground black pepper

4 ice cubes

SERVES 4

1 Pinch out the green tops from the strawberries with your fingers or cut off the tops with a small knife. Put the fruit into a blender, then add the yoghurt, honey and herbs. Add a pinch of salt and about 3 grinds of the pepper mill.

2 ASK AN ADULT TO HELP YOU blend the mixture very briefly so the fruit becomes a thick, coarse purée rather than a smooth milkshake. Taste and add more honey, pepper or salt if you like – the soup should not taste sweet.

3 If serving right away, stir in the ice cubes and serve in chilled bowls with a sprig of mint or basil on top.

4 If taking it to school, pour the mixture into individual vacuum flasks, then add an ice cube to each one. Stir gently before eating.

5 The soup can also be stored in a jug, tightly covered, overnight in the refrigerator.

websites and mail order

Equipment and Utensils

Books for Cooks
4 Blenheim Crescent
Notting Hill
London W11 1NN
Tel: 020 7221 1992
Fax: 020 7221 1517
Email: info@booksforcooks.com
www.booksforcooks.com
*Wonderful shop open Tuesday to
Saturday, 10 am to 6 pm (closed
August and Christmas), selling
every cookbook you'll ever want,
plus light lunches and cooking
classes. Cookbooks by post too.*

Cucina Direct
PO Box 6611
London SW15 2WG
Tel: 020 8246 4300
Fax: 020 8246 4330
www.cucinadirect.co.uk
*Interesting selection of mail order
cooking and kitchen equipment,
telephone for catalogue or
browse online.*

David Mellor
4 Sloane Street
London SWI 8EE
Tel: 020 7730 4259
www.davidmellordesign.co.uk
*Well-stocked shop plus mail
order catalogue.*

Divertimenti
139–141 Fulham Road
London SW3 6SD
Tel: 020 7581 8065
Fax: 020 7823 9429
33–34 Marylebone High Street
London W1U 4PT
Tel: 020 7935 0689
www.divertimenti.co.uk
*Two shops in London plus
comprehensive mail order
catalogue for equipment.*

Lakeland Ltd
Alexandra Buildings
Windermere
Cumbria LA23 1BQ
Tel: 015394 88100
Fax: 015394 88300
www.lakelandlimited.com
*Huge range of high quality, good
value cooking equipment and
some hard-to-find ingredients.
Look out for the pasta machine,
waffle cooker, microwave popcorn
maker and small-scale mixing
bowls, knives, peelers etc. as well
as essentials like oven gloves.
Available by mail order, online and
from their shops. Fast and friendly
service – phone for a catalogue.*

Silverwood Limited
Ledsam House
Ledsam Street
Birmingham B16 8DN
Tel: 0121 454 3571/2
Fax: 0121 454 6749
Email: sales@alan-
silverwood.co.uk
*Professional quality bakeware
(bread and cake tins, brownie
tins, baking trays, etc.) designed
to last rather longer than your
oven. Aga range available too.
Stocked by Lakeland, John Lewis
stores, major department stores
and good cook shops. For local
stockists, phone for details.*

Cooking Classes

Bettys Cookery School
Hookstone Park
Hookstone Chase
Harrogate
North Yorkshire HG2 7LD
Tel: 01423 814016
www.bettyscookeryschool.co.uk
*Purpose-built cooking school at
Starbeck with wide range of
1-day courses. Also, half-term
and Saturday classes for children
aged 8 to 10, 11 to 13 and
14 to 16 (the children can take
home what they bake).*

The Kids' Cookery School
107 Gunnersbury Lane
Acton
London W3 8HQ
Tel: 020 8992 8882
Fax: 020 8992 7770
Email:
info@thekidscookeryschool.co.uk
www.thekidscookeryschool.co.uk
*For children aged 3 to 16. Small
classes and inspiring teachers
bring out the best in every child
and instil great confidence. Food
Therapy Afterschool Club, half-
term and school holiday classes
and workshops, and school class
visits. Registered charity, non-
profit making.*

Yeast

Fresh yeast is available from the
bakery counter of in-store bakeries
in larger supermarkets, and some
wholefood/organic food stores.

Herb, Vegetable and Salad Seeds

Halcyon Seeds
10 Hampden Close
Chalgrove
Oxfordshire OX44 7SB
Tel: 01865 890180
*Encourage children to grow their
own ingredients with this
catalogue service.*

Marshalls Vegetable Seed Company
SE Marshalls & Co Ltd.
Freepost PE787
Wisbech
Cambs PE13 2WE
Tel: 01945 466711
*All you need for your own family
kitchen garden.*

index